CW01337846

St Antony's Series
General Editor: **Eugene Rogan** (1997–), Fellow of St Antony's College, Oxford

Recent titles include:

Carl Aaron
THE POLITICAL ECONOMY OF JAPANESE FOREIGN DIRECT INVESTMENT IN THE UK AND THE US

Uri Bialer
OIL AND THE ARAB–ISRAELI CONFLICT, 1948–63

Craig Brandist and Galin Tihanov (*editors*)
MATERIALIZING BAKHTIN

Mark Brzezinski
THE STRUGGLE FOR CONSTITUTIONALISM IN POLAND

Reinhard Drifte
JAPAN'S QUEST FOR A PERMANENT SECURITY COUNCIL SEAT
A Matter of Pride or Justice?

Simon Duke
THE ELUSIVE QUEST FOR EUROPEAN SECURITY

Tim Dunne
INVENTING INTERNATIONAL SOCIETY

Marta Dyczok
THE GRAND ALLIANCE AND UKRAINIAN REFUGEES

Ken Endo
THE PRESIDENCY OF THE EUROPEAN COMMISSION UNDER JACQUES DELORS

M. K. Flynn
IDEOLOGY, MOBILIZATION AND THE NATION
The Rise of Irish, Basque and Carlist Nationalist Movements in the Nineteenth and Early Twentieth Centuries

Anthony Forster
BRITAIN AND THE MAASTRICHT NEGOTIATIONS

Ricardo Ffrench-Davis
REFORMING THE REFORMS IN LATIN AMERICA
Macroeconomics, Trade, Finance

Azar Gat
BRITISH ARMOUR THEORY AND THE RISE OF THE PANZER ARM
Revising the Revisionists

Fernando Guirao
SPAIN AND THE RECONSTRUCTION OF WESTERN EUROPE, 1945–57

Anthony Kirk-Greene
BRITAIN'S IMPERIAL ADMINISTRATORS, 1858–1966

Bernardo Kosacoff
CORPORATE STRATEGIES UNDER STRUCTURAL ADJUSTMENT IN ARGENTINA
Responses by Industrial Firms to a New Set of Uncertainties

Huck-ju Kwon
THE WELFARE STATE IN KOREA

Cécile Laborde
PLURALIST THOUGHT IN BRITAIN AND FRANCE, 1900–25

Eiichi Motono
CONFLICT AND COOPERATION IN SINO–BRITISH BUSINESS, 1860–1911
The Impact of the Pro-British Commercial Network in Shanghai

C. S. Nicholls
THE HISTORY OF ST ANTONY'S COLLEGE, OXFORD, 1950–2000

Laila Parsons
THE DRUZE BETWEEN PALESTINE AND ISRAEL, 1947–49

Shane O'Rourke
WARRIORS AND PEASANTS
The Don Cossacks in Late Imperial Russia

Patricia Sloane
ISLAM, MODERNITY AND ENTREPRENEURSHIP AMONG THE MALAYS

Karina Sonnenberg-Stern
EMANCIPATION AND POVERTY
The Ashkenazi Jews of Amsterdam, 1796–1850

Miguel Székely
THE ECONOMICS OF POVERTY AND WEALTH ACCUMULATION IN MEXICO

Ray Takeyh
THE ORIGINS OF THE EISENHOWER DOCTRINE
The US, Britain and Nasser's Egypt, 1953–57

Steve Tsang and Hung-mao Tien (*editors*)
DEMOCRATIZATION IN TAIWAN

Yongjin Zhang
CHINA IN INTERNATIONAL SOCIETY SINCE 1949

Jan Zielonka
EXPLAINING EURO-PARALYSIS

St Antony's Series
Series Standing Order ISBN 0–333–71109–2
(*outside North America only*)

You can receive future titles in this series as they are published by placing a standing order. Please contact your bookseller or, in case of difficulty, write to us at the address below with your name and address, the title of the series and the ISBN quoted above.

Customer Services Department, Macmillan Distribution Ltd, Houndmills, Basingstoke, Hampshire RG21 6XS, England

British Armour Theory and the Rise of the Panzer Arm

Revising the Revisionists

Azar Gat
Associate Professor and Chairman
Department of Political Science
Tel Aviv University
Israel

in association with
ST ANTONY'S COLLEGE, OXFORD

First published in Great Britain 2000 by
MACMILLAN PRESS LTD
Houndmills, Basingstoke, Hampshire RG21 6XS and London
Companies and representatives throughout the world

A catalogue record for this book is available from the British Library.

ISBN 0–333–77348–9

First published in the United States of America 2000 by
ST. MARTIN'S PRESS, INC.,
Scholarly and Reference Division,
175 Fifth Avenue, New York, N.Y. 10010

ISBN 0–312–22952–6

Library of Congress Cataloging-in-Publication Data
Gat, Azar.
British armour theory and the rise of the Panzer Arm : revising the revisionists / Azar Gat.
p. cm.
Includes bibliographical references and index.
ISBN 0–312–22952–6 (cloth)
1. Tank warfare. 2. Liddell Hart, Basil Henry, Sir, 1895–1970. 3. Germany. Heer—Armored troops. I. Title.

UE159 .G33 1999
358'.18'0904—dc21

99–046107

© Azar Gat 2000

All rights reserved. No reproduction, copy or transmission of this publication may be made without written permission.

No paragraph of this publication may be reproduced, copied or transmitted save with written permission or in accordance with the provisions of the Copyright, Designs and Patents Act 1988, or under the terms of any licence permitting limited copying issued by the Copyright Licensing Agency, 90 Tottenham Court Road, London W1P 0LP.

Any person who does any unauthorised act in relation to this publication may be liable to criminal prosecution and civil claims for damages.

The author has asserted his right to be identified as the author of this work in accordance with the Copyright, Designs and Patents Act 1988.

This book is printed on paper suitable for recycling and made from fully managed and sustained forest sources.

10   9   8   7   6   5   4   3   2   1
09   08   07   06   05   04   03   02   01   00

Printed and bound in Great Britain by
Antony Rowe Ltd, Chippenham, Wiltshire

To Ruthie

Contents

Preface		viii
Acknowledgements		xi
1	**Liddell Hart's Theory of Armoured Warfare**	1
i	Deep strategic penetration	5
ii	Combating 'Blitzkrieg'	18
iii	The all-arms armoured formation	35
2	**British Influence and the Evolution of the Panzer Arm**	43
I	Origins: the 1920s and early 1930s	49
II	The creation of the Panzer arm	68
Conclusion		91
Notes		96
Select Bibliography		119
Index		124

Preface

This book grew from my work on another. Among the main themes of *Fascist and Liberal Visions of War: Fuller, Liddell Hart, Douhet and Other Modernists* (1998), the third volume of my cultural history trilogy of modern strategic thought, was the evolution, cross-nationally, of the theory of mechanized warfare from the beginning of the twentieth century. In the main, what I wrote there will not be repeated here. However, as I was writing that book it became clear to me that some recent scholarly trends in the study of crucial historical questions, such as the evolution of British armour theory during the interwar period, the influence of the British school on the Germans, and the genesis of the Panzer arm itself, are in need of a major reassessment. The broad cultural perspective of *Fascist and Liberal Visions of War* did not allow the space required for such a detailed reassessment. A separate volume has become necessary.

The questions mentioned above are inseparably historical as well as historiographical in nature. With respect to both Britain and Germany the historiography of the theory and practice of armoured warfare during the interwar period was written, and wholly dominated, by the armour enthusiasts themselves, whose version of events held sway in scholarly and popular accounts for more than a generation. Major-General J.F.C. Fuller and B.H. Liddell Hart were the leading theorists, brilliant propagandists, and flamboyant historians who captured most of the limelight in Britain. Liddell Hart further enhanced his hold over history through his post-Second World War association with the creators of the Panzer arm, most notably Heinz Guderian, whose own memoirs dominated the historiography of German armour. It is only since the 1970s, when these towering figures were no longer around and as both the British and German archives became available to scholars, that the armour enthusiasts' monopoly over the historiography has been broken and their interpretation challenged. In respect to both Britain and Germany they have been criticized on similar grounds: there were vast gaps in their visions; they were dogmatic in advocating their ideas of mechanization and were blind to anything that stood in the way, such as higher political considerations, strategic priorities, and economic constraints; their polemic zeal and highly subjective approaches caricatured their perceived opponents and distorted the latter's arguments; their egocentric personalities made them disproportionately concentrate everything around themselves.

This process of critical reevaluation has been more than necessary. As scholars have replaced protagonists and documentary history has taken the place of memoirs, our understanding of the development of the theory of armoured warfare in both Britain and Germany has been put on a wholly different footing and gained much in depth. Unfortunately, however, in some respects criticism has gone astray. The main cause of this was the problem of Liddell Hart. Even more than other armour enthusiasts, doubts regarding his accuracy, and indeed honesty, began to surface after his death in 1970. Since his version of events concerning British armour theory, influence on the Germans, and German theory and practice had been predominant, much of the accepted historical picture came into question. In particular, John Mearsheimer's devastating *Liddell Hart and the Weight of History* (1988) developed the question-marks into a far-reaching revision that has become accepted by many.

As this book will attempt to show, the principal conclusions of this revision were mostly erroneous. For all of its many shortcomings, the traditional interpretation was not as far from the truth as it has recently become the fashion to believe. As we shall see, on the whole, Britain was indeed the source of the modern theory of armoured warfare and a model for all armies, most significantly the German. Fuller and Liddell Hart did play a prominent role in these developments both at home and abroad.

This book, then, is a monograph about the evolution and diffusion of a strategic doctrine in Britain and Germany during the interwar period. *Fascist and Liberal Visions of War* has already dealt with some of the broader aspects of mechanization, with Fuller's conception of mechanized warfare and with his and Liddell Hart's overall theory of war and historical significance. Thus, concentrating on the main points of contention, the first study of this book focuses on Liddell Hart's theory of armoured warfare. His own account of it, as well as the revisionist critique, have between them been responsible for a great deal of confusion regarding British armour developments during the interwar period. In view of Liddell Hart's pivotal historical and, no less, historiographical role, his ideas serve here as a prism, through which the evolution of British armour thinking and of the British armoured forces during the interwar period is refracted.

The book's treatment of the German scene widens the focus further. While *Fascist and Liberal Visions of War* dealt with the general modernist ideological and political aspects of German mechanization, the second study of this book attempts to reconstruct an overall picture of the evolution of the Panzer arm, with special emphasis on the British influence on this process. Although a highly popular subject, the evolution of the Panzer arm has received surprisingly little serious documentary study and is still largely shrouded in myths and counter-myths. Furthermore, although the link between interwar British and German armour developments used to be accepted as crucial, these developments have never been studied conjointly in a scholarly way. The concentration on the two countries which have traditionally been regarded as pivotal in the development of the doctrine of armoured warfare does not, of course, deny the significance of other countries, most notably the Soviet Union (discussed in *Fascist and Liberal Visions of War*). It is simply that the long-established 'core story' of armour doctrine has been called into question, and the record has to be reevaluated and put right.

Acknowledgements

During my work on this book in two countries I have incurred many pleasant debts to people and institutions that have lent me their help and support. In Germany I was hosted by Miltärgeschichtliches Forschungsamt, then in Freiburg i. Breisgau. I am particularly grateful to the Institute's former Chief Historian, Professor Wilhelm Deist, who patiently and tactfully guided my steps into interwar German military history. In addition, the warm friendship and hospitality which Professor and Frau Deist extended to my family and myself made our stays in Freiburg even more rewarding. In Britain my mentor, Professor Sir Michael Howard, as well as Professors Brian Bond and Robert O'Neill, shared with me their views and some personal recollections of Liddell Hart. Needless to say, the views expressed and the errors that still remain in this book are my responsibility alone.

Of the libraries and archives consulted in the course of my research, I am particularly thankful to the staffs of the Liddell Hart Centre for Military Archives at King's College, London, and of the Bundes Archiv-Militär Archiv, Freiburg, for their dedicated and patient service. The Trustees of the Liddell Hart Centre for Military Archives kindly gave me permission to cite from documents to which they hold copyright. I am also thankful to *War in History* and the *Journal of Strategic Studies* for allowing me to use material first published in these periodicals. Finally, my research was made possible by the generous support of the Alexander von Humboldt Foundation and the British Council. I am most grateful to both.

1
Liddell Hart's Theory of Armoured Warfare

Sir Basil Henry Liddell Hart's fame rests largely on his perceived role as a leading, if not *the* leading, theorist of modern armoured warfare. During the interwar period he supposedly envisaged, developed, and directly influenced the way armoured forces would be employed during the Second World War, first by the Germans in their brilliant 'Blitzkrieg' campaigns and, subsequently, by all other major armies. Yet in recent years historians have come to doubt and reject this picture, arguing that Liddell Hart (1895–1970) largely fabricated the accepted image of his role in, and influence upon, the development of the doctrine of armoured warfare. The consequences for his reputation have been devastating. Highly egocentric and vain, Liddell Hart carries much of the blame for this change of opinion. His almost compulsive manipulations of evidence for the purpose of self-aggrandizement could not in the long run withstand critical scrutiny and only cast doubt on everything he wrote about himself. Nonetheless, a further examination of the evidence reveals that the main charges levelled against him are misplaced and based on almost incredible historiographical slips on the part of his chief critic, John Mearsheimer. Indeed, once the distortions created by himself and by others are removed, the picture that emerges is not very far from the accepted one and is, on the whole, impressive as far as Liddell Hart is concerned.

A humble young captain struggling to remain in the post war British army and already an innovative expert on infantry training, drill and tactics, Liddell Hart was converted to the idea of armoured warfare by J.F.C. Fuller in 1922. Yet in later years Liddell Hart would strive to minimize his debt and join himself as closely as possible and in an independent role to the earliest tank pioneers. In his *Memoirs* (1965) he misleadingly presented an article he had published in 1919 in the

Journal of the Royal United Services Institution as evidence that he had begun to regard the tank as the paramount arm of the future immediately after the First World War. He did not mention the title of that article, 'Suggestions on the Future Development of the Combat Unit – the Tank as a Weapon of Infantry', which would have betrayed the wholly traditional and uninspiring nature of his suggestions, made in connection with his preoccupation at that time with infantry minor tactics. To make the matter all the more ironical, there was a contemporary critic who wrote to him that it would be a mistake to tie up the tanks to infantry and thus slow them down.[1] Also in a traditional vein, in a sharp critique of H.G. Wells' end-of-the-war prophecies regarding the future of mechanization, Liddell Hart denied that the days of cavalry were over.[2]

Although much later Liddell Hart would have the nerve to write to Fuller that he had discovered that his conversion to armoured warfare had begun before he had met Fuller,[3] the evidence in the matter is abundantly clear. Not long after they had made contact in 1920, the then Colonel Fuller (1878–1965) – GSO 1 of the Tank Corps during the First World War and Britain's recognized leading tank expert – told Liddell Hart, who was consulting him about his work on the new British infantry manual, that the tank and not infantry was the means to penetrate entrenched fronts.[4] By the end of and immediately after the war Fuller had already developed his vision of fully mechanized armies that would dominate future war.[5] For some time, however, the main subject in the Fuller–Liddell Hart correspondence was the principles and science of war, in which both of them were interested, and it was only in early 1922 that things came to a head in their more strictly professional fields. In a short exchange which developed from Fuller's comments on the draft of the 'Infantry' article which Liddell Hart was writing in General Sir Ivor Maxse's name for the *Encyclopedia Britannica*, Fuller shook and broke down Liddell Hart's faith in the continuing leading role of infantry on the battlefields of the future. In his note of surrender Liddell Hart wrote: 'Your arguments are so convincing on the tank v. other arms as they exist, that I am fain to become a disciple ... may I ask what are the possibilities of a transfer to the Tank Corps?'[6] He continued to publish articles on infantry that year, but now assumed that this arm must find its future within a predominantly mechanized battlefield.[7] Soon he was to move to the new field altogether.

The new stage in Liddell Hart's thought was opened with an essay, 'The Next Great War', which he wrote in late 1922 for the first Royal

United Services Institution competition to be announced after the one Fuller had won in 1919. The essay failed to win the prize, but not necessarily because of a conservative backlash, as Fuller and Liddell Hart suggested.[8] The judges' decision not to select the same work twice in a row is understandable – Liddell Hart's essay was almost a replica of Fuller's. In the introductory part he reproduced Fuller's vision of future war based on the expansion of scientific civilization into the battlefield in the shape of the tank, the airplane and gas. As Fuller had done, he demonstrated the superiority of the new arms over the old by a clumsy scholastic analysis in the light of Fuller's principles. This part he would publish separately, under the original title, in 1924.[9] The more substantial part of Liddell Hart's essay, also published in 1924 and entitled 'The Development of the "New Model" Army, Suggestions on a Progressive, but Gradual, Mechanization', was considerably more mature but was similarly based on the ideas of Fuller's gold-medal work. Only the phases of mechanization, (which were obviously largely arbitrary) were somewhat differently worked out. During Liddell Hart's first, evolutionary, period of mechanization, the division's transport, artillery and infantry would be mechanized in successive stages, while its manpower was reduced. Each of the three brigades in the division would consist of three infantry battalions, one mechanized artillery battalion, one heavy assault, and one lighter, mopping-up, tank battalion. In addition, the divisional level would include one battalion of independent pursuit tanks, one battalion of bridge-tanks and one battalion of gas-tanks. In the second, revolutionary, period, which would be dominated by the tank and the airplane, the division would become fully armoured, and all its elements would possess cross-country mobility. It would operate from fortified bases which it would form along its route.[10]

Liddell Hart again produced a Fullerite picture of future mechanized warfare in *Paris, or the Future of War* (1925), which plagiarized Fuller's *The Reformation of War* (1923) – 'the book of the century' in Liddell Hart's admiring words – almost lock, stock and barrel, without any acknowledgement.[11] Air power using the humane and non-destructive gas would dominate war, overwhelming in a very short period the enemy's civilian rear as well as immobilizing the old, obsolete mass armies. Concentrated armoured forces would travel the countryside, operating against the enemy's command and communications, his 'nerve system', in the manner Fuller had suggested in 1918. In the naval arena it would seem that at least in closed seas the aircraft and the submarine would displace the battleship.[12]

This was Fuller almost to the letter. To remove any doubt, we are not dealing here with ideas developed conjointly; nor do we have here two lines of thought running parallel, as Liddell Hart would claim in later years.[13] A comparative examination of the development of Fuller and Liddell Hart respectively clearly reveals that the ideas which Fuller had developed by 1922–23 – not only regarding armoured warfare but in many other respects – came as a revelation to the admiring Liddell Hart, who made them his own.[14]

Liddell Hart continued his advocacy of mechanization in his collection of articles, *The Remaking of Modern Armies* (1927). His appointment in 1925, after his discharge from the army, as the military correspondent of *The Daily Telegraph* – until the mid-1930s the only newspaper in Britain to employ such a correspondent on a permanent basis – gave him an influential platform from which he would relentlessly champion the cause of mechanization. In the following years, like Fuller, he would rapidly win a national and international renown as a military theorist, critic and historian.

All this raises an obvious question: apart from being a skilful, popular and well-connected propagandist of mechanization, what, if any, beyond the vision and ideas he adopted from Fuller, were Liddell Hart's own contributions to the theory of armoured warfare? After presenting his early writings on the subject in his *Memoirs*, Liddell Hart addressed this question with the following oft-cited passages:

> Fuller had come by now to think that the tank alone would dominate future battlefields, and that infantry would not be needed except to garrison the country that the tanks had conquered. On the other hand I argued that there was both need and scope for a more mobile kind of infantry to co-operate with the tanks in an armoured force, and form part of it, for prompt aid in overcoming defended obstacles. I visualised them as what I called 'tank marines', carried in armoured vehicles along with the land fleet – or, putting it another way, as mechanized 'mounted infantry' ... In short, Fuller concentrated on the development of an all-tank army, while I favoured an all-mobile army – in which all the tank-aiding arms would be mounted in armoured vehicles, and thus able to accompany the tanks closely....
>
> Another difference of view was over the way of using an armoured force in exploiting a breach in the enemy's defence. For, while Fuller brilliantly expounded from 1918 onward the idea of a *deep*

tactical penetration, he did not advocate the *deep strategic penetration*, as I did. He favoured the armoured forces being used for a manoeuvre against the opposing army's immediate rear, rather than against its communications far in the rear. Thus he preferred an advance by fairly long but limited bounds, instead of driving on as fast and as far as possible – which became my concept when developing for armoured forces the 'expanding torrent' method.[15]

Both points were, obviously, of crucial significance, for in both cases it was with Liddell Hart's rather than with Fuller's ideas that the organization and practice of the German Panzer forces during the Second World War would be associated.

i. Deep strategic penetration

However, in recent years historians have come to suspect and reject all of Liddell Hart's claims regarding his ideas and influence. In the first place, from which much of the rest follow, it has been alleged that during the interwar period he never advocated the idea of deep strategic penetration by armoured forces, the hallmark of the future 'Blitzkrieg'. In his *Memoirs*, if only by association, Liddell Hart gave the impression that this idea could be found in his early essay and derivative articles of 1922–24.[16] But as we have seen, and as Mearsheimer has already pointed out, that essay did not go beyond a call for mechanization, the advancement of organizational schemes, and Fuller's ideas. Furthermore, Mearsheimer has pointed out that Liddell Hart never wrote a systematic treatise outlining his conception of future mechanized warfare. He has argued that Liddell Hart's references to the subject were scarce, were made mostly in the 1920s, and ceased almost completely in the 1930s. Comparing Liddell Hart's ideas in those years with the way the Germans were to practise 'Blitzkrieg' in the Second World War, Mearsheimer has admitted that Liddell Hart remarkably anticipated most of the salient features of future developments: he clearly regarded the tank, operating in concentrated formations and aided by other arms and by close air support, as the decisive instrument of war; he envisaged armoured formations, flexibly led by a system of forward command, piercing the enemy's front and operating in its rear to create dislocation and collapse. Still, argued Mearsheimer, the idea of *deep* strategic drives, essential to the Germans' shattering successes during the early phases of the Second World War, cannot be found in Liddell Hart's interwar writings.

Mearsheimer has thus concluded that Liddell Hart's claim that he had advocated the idea of deep armoured penetration was born only *after* the Second World War and in the wake of the German successes. He has argued that in the absence of any real evidence to support his claim, Liddell Hart misleadingly cited in his *Memoirs* his studies of Mongol strategy and of Sherman's campaigns and his concepts of the 'expanding torrent' and of the 'indirect approach', none of which had ever related to his published ideas on the use of armoured forces.[17]

Earlier historians had in fact encountered the same problem. Jay Luvaas noted that before the Second World War Liddell Hart 'did not often mention *deep* strategic penetration as such'.[18] Brian Bond, whose book on Liddell Hart did not deal with the latter's theory of armoured warfare at any significant length, has expressed the opinion that Mearsheimer's allegation was correct. In a conversation with the author of this book he recalled that in the early 1960s a German doctoral student had written to Liddell Hart, asking where exactly in his writings he had advocated deep strategic penetration. Bond, Liddell Hart's neighbour, protégé and informal research assistant, was asked by Liddell Hart to fetch the relevant material from the latter's archive but failed to locate any, arousing an impatient response from Liddell Hart.[19]

All this seems to be so much in character with Liddell Hart as to appear almost certainly true, but in fact it is not. Historians have looked in the wrong places. They have searched Liddell Hart's books and magazine articles, which would have normally been sufficient, for he habitually and endlessly reprocessed and rehashed his writings, using and reusing material he had initially written for newspapers in his magazine articles and again in his books. By a curious accident, however, this pattern did not occur here. The bulk of Liddell Hart's ideas concerning the theory of armoured warfare appeared in his regular columns in *The Daily Telegraph* (and from 1935 *The Times*), and a great deal of it has never been reprinted.[20] For a decade in the summers from 1927 on Britain intermittently experimented with the world's first brigade-size, independent mechanized formation, in the forming of which the propagandist endeavour of Fuller and Liddell Hart had played a prominent role.[21] The manoeuvres deployed the world's first operational long-range and fast tank, the Vickers Medium. Attending and covering these manoeuvres, which were eagerly watched by the experts and general staffs of all the major armies, Liddell Hart developed in his *Daily Telegraph* columns the most brilliant and prophetic blueprint offered at the time of the way armoured warfare would be practised in the opening stages of the Second World War.

The experimental mechanized force, assembled during the summer of 1927, started its first trials on Salisbury Plain on 19 August. Like the other armour enthusiasts Liddell Hart was elated by the realization of a dream but criticized the mixed composition of the force whose component parts, scraped together from existing units and employing widely varying and obsolescent equipment, found it difficult to co-operate effectively. The radicals were also disappointed by what they regarded as too conservative guidelines laid down for the trials. On 31 August Liddell Hart wrote from the field:

> We seem to have got away from the idea of trying out the potentialities of a force of armoured fighting vehicles capable of wide strategic manoeuvre and of restoring the lost master-key of surprise. Instead we have seen the 'mechanized' force functioning as if it were merely the tactical limb of an ordinary division.[22]

On 8 September 1927, Sir George Milne, the Chief of the Imperial General Staff and for a time the hero of the armour enthusiasts as the man who very much under the persuasion of Fuller and Liddell Hart had initiated the experimental mechanized force, summarized the trials in his Tidworth address. To the thrill of the radicals he promised future armoured divisions. Eloquence was not one of Milne's strong points, and the address was anyhow drafted for him by one of the armour activists, Lieutenant-Colonel Charles Broad, then SD2 at the general staff, and was based entirely on the vision and ideas of Fuller and Liddell Hart. Among the passages which derived more specifically from the latter's rhetoric one reads:

> It is the great cavalry raids by people like the Mongols and Parthians, where there was nothing to stop the action of cavalry, that want your consideration. There you have cavalry living on the country and travelling long distances. You have the absolute acme of strategic mobility in the theatres of operations and that is the sort of mobility I want you to study.... A force of this description you can use as a swinging blow to come around the flank. It is an armoured force intended for long distance work. It may be necessary to employ it as an armoured force for close work, but essentially what I am aiming at is a mobile armoured force that can go long distances and carry out big operations and big turning movements.[23]

Admittedly, most of Liddell Hart's many references to Mongol medieval cavalry warfare in relation to modern mechanized warfare concerned tactics. They were mostly made in connection with questions like the mixing of light and medium tanks in the tank companies and battalions and the carrying out of battle drills by signals. Yet, from the start, Liddell Hart primarily emphasized the Mongols' strategic mobility, logistic self-sufficiency, and role as the pioneers of 'strategic convergence' as a model for future mechanized forces.[24] More important still, in 1928 Liddell Hart wrote *Sherman* and *The Decisive Wars of History* (later renamed *Strategy: the Indirect Approach*), and while these books certainly did not deal specifically with mechanized warfare, their main theme was the superiority of strategy and the variety of means at its disposal over tactics and the clash of forces. Indeed this became Liddell Hart's leading idea in the sphere of field warfare. Thus, even before examining the evidence, it should have been clear that the claim that Liddell Hart advocated the tactical but not the strategic use of armoured forces runs counter to the entire drift and logic of his thought in those years and ever after. In fact, he relentlessly preached little else.

Summarizing the trials of 1927, again during the manoeuvres of the redesignated Armoured Force in the following summer and often later, Liddell Hart argued that mobility, not fire-power, was the force's major asset, and that it ought to manoeuvre and repeatedly emerge in unexpected places with a view of disorienting and paralysing the enemy rather than fight to destroy him in battle.[25] He called for calculated dispersion and, indeed, for 'indirect approach'.[26] He stressed that 'the strategic attack on the enemy's line of communications and retreat is the true role for such a force.'[27] He maintained that as long as the armoured force remained small its main use would necessarily be restricted to raids rather than to a truly decisive, war-winning, cutting of communications, and that it was therefore essential that the force should be expanded.[28] He claimed that the policy of general mechanization of the infantry and cavalry, announced when the experimental force was disbanded to the dismay of the armour enthusiasts after the manoeuvres of 1928, was no substitute for specialized armoured divisions.[29] Only 'armoured forces, future armoured divisions ... provide the Commander in Chief of our Expeditionary Force with a strategic thrusting weapon', which he would be able to use 'for wide and rapid manoeuvre beyond the range of ordinary manoeuvre'.[30]

Liddell Hart also discussed his conception of armoured warfare in several magazine articles he published in 1929 and 1930, but to the bedevilment of historians he did not specifically use the term 'strategic' manoeuvre in those articles, just 'wide manoeuvre and the attack on the enemy's rear' and 'lines of supply'.[31] No brigade-size armour manoeuvres were held in 1929, and a year later only a reduced armoured brigade participated in the summer exercises and was employed in co-operation with horse cavalry and infantry rather than in an independent role. In the view of the radicals this was a serious and regrettable step backwards. All the same, in reviewing the 1930 manoeuvres, Liddell Hart had to lower his sights somewhat, criticizing the neglect of raids on the model of the American Civil War on 'strategic' targets such as communications and depots and the fact that the tanks were directed against the enemy's front rather than for 'a blow at the enemy's headquarters, signal centres, transport lines, and supply columns.'[32]

In 1931 an armoured brigade was again assembled under Charles Broad's command and successfully tried out for the first time a system of radio control. Following another successful training season in the summer of 1932, a decision to create a permanent armoured brigade was finally accepted in 1933. The exercises in 1931–32 did not go beyond the tactical employment of armour and, while Liddell Hart was delighted with the progress made, he continued to call for more far-reaching conduct. On the basis of the final manoeuvres of the 1932 season, in which the armoured brigade was offered a freer hand and 'as a whole was used as an army's strategic arm of manoeuvre', he drew attention to the fact that even a manoeuvre of 250–300 miles was now logistically feasible.[33] 'Fast tanks are best used independently for real strategic strokes – such as wide manoeuvres against enemy's communications.'[34]

The 1934 summer manoeuvres were a historical landmark in the development of mechanized warfare. For the first time large-scale, deep armoured strategic penetrations were tried out by the newly formed 1st Tank Brigade, commanded by Brigadier Percy Hobart. The brigade's mandate was to 'be employed on a strategic or semi-independent mission against some important objective in the enemy's rearward organization.... The Tank Brigade should avoid strength and attack weakness.' It was to 'aim at moving seventy miles in a day or 150 miles in three days, including an action in either case.'[35] The evidence suggests that Liddell Hart did not exaggerate his involvement in, and contribution to, the shaping of the concept which underlay the manoeuvres.[36] He and Hobart were keeping, and would continue to keep for more than a decade, an intensive and intimate exchange of views and information from which both of them benefited greatly. Hobart sought, assimilated and codified Liddell Hart's ideas while sharing with him his unrivalled professional knowledge, proficiency and expertise;[37] from 1934 to the outbreak of the Second World War he was Britain's leading authority on armoured warfare. Liddell Hart's finger-prints are detectable all over the Tank Brigade Report:

> the deeper behind the Battle Zone that the Tank Brigade could penetrate the more widespread would be the confusion and dislocation it would cause, and the more effective would be its action. Moreover the deeper it went the safer it would be....
>
> It must, therefore, move rapidly and be able to appear and disappear. It must avoid unnecessary losses. It must be very flexible and controllable and continually manoeuvre so as to threaten a number of objectives. It must induce enemy concentrations in one direction and then suddenly move sixty or seventy miles elsewhere. It must be able to strike rapidly, carrying out effective destruction in two or three hours and withdraw rapidly and leave the enemy uncertain of its exact whereabouts. It must be able to disperse into small columns in order to mislead the enemy and re-unite as required; it must be capable of completely controlled movement both by day and night.[38]

Describing the 'strategic move' of the previous day's exercise to the readers of *The Daily Telegraph*, Liddell Hart wrote that it had 'proved beyond doubt the possibility of a tank force making an effective move of a hundred miles in the twenty-four hours ... '[39]

The Army Training Memorandum No. 13, issued in December 1934 and signed by the CIGS since 1933, Sir Archibald Montgomery-Massingberd, recognized both the use of the Tank Brigade for the 'strategic role against some distant objective' and its 'major tactical role'. For the next year's training season the memorandum laid down that the Tank Brigade was to be 'mainly directed to actions in or close to the main battle'.[40] In the 1935 manoeuvres themselves Hobart did, however, succeed in carrying out some deep armoured strokes. Yet Liddell Hart's criticism of the brigade's manoeuvre again highlights the distinctive nature of what he regarded as an 'independent strategic role':

> After using its strategic mobility to circle northward round the flank of the opposing army ... it was directed southward into the

'tactical zone' of that army in order to aid the offensive of its own army by direct interference with the enemy withdrawal and the movements of his reserves. The value of such assistance is obvious, perhaps too obvious. Whether it is the most valuable service that such a force can perform, and whether the prospective reward justifies the risk ... are questions that remain. An army has to be fed by rail and road, and in the light of historical experience, it would seem that the Tank Brigade might be more effectively and less riskily employed in severing these vital arteries.... Analysis also suggests that the farther back a mobile stroke is aimed, the greater is apt to be the effect, and the less the risk of the stroke itself being interrupted.

'Armies', he complained, 'always tended to be tactically, rather than strategically minded.'[41]

All this striking but strangely elusive and unquoted material is sufficient to demonstrate the falsity of the assertions that 'there is no evidence ... that Liddell Hart understood the importance of the deep strategic penetration *before* World War II ... much less called attention to it'; ' ... this was not an issue among British armour advocates at the time.'[42] Students of British armoured doctrine, familiar with the development of the armoured force and particularly with Hobart's historical manoeuvres in 1934–37 could not, and mostly did not, make such mistakes. Unfortunately, the relevant references in their works have also been missed by Liddell Hart's critic.[43] Thus, ironically, Liddell Hart wins a full score precisely by the way his critic has framed the problem. The very idea he has marked as the central feature of the future 'Blitzkrieg' and has alleged Liddell Hart failed to uphold is in fact revealed to be Liddell Hart's major thesis in the field of armoured warfare during the interwar period.

There remains, of course, the question why, as was his habit in other parts of his *Memoirs*, Liddell Hart did not quote extensively from his writings at the time in order to demonstrate rather than merely state his position regarding deep strategic penetration. The answer to this would appear to be fairly trivial. In the chapters dealing with armoured warfare in his *Memoirs* Liddell Hart mostly rehashed material he had written for his major study *The Tanks*, published six years before his *Memoirs*. Now, in *The Tanks*, a subscribers' book commissioned by the veterans of the Royal Tank Regiment, Liddell Hart made a noticeable effort not to occupy the scene entirely for himself, as was normally his habit.[44] With this in view he also avoided lengthy quotations from his own works. Obviously, he did not imagine that anyone would doubt his key position during the interwar period regarding the strategic use of armoured forces, a position which was well known to the veterans of the Tank Corps.

But let us return to the development of Liddell Hart's theory of deep strategic armoured operations. The assumption laid down for Hobart's 1934 manoeuvres was that in case of war, as in 1914, a British expeditionary force would operate to the left of the French army against a German invasion of the Low Countries and northern France. Within that scenario it was envisaged that the armoured force would utilize the open north-western flank for a wide enveloping manoeuvre against the enemy's rear.[45] However, in the second half of the 1930s Liddell Hart correctly assessed that there might not be an open flank to exploit on the western front. Therefore, he now increasingly stressed that the armoured forces' strategic leverage on the enemy can be exerted either 'by enveloping his flank or by putting pressure on an inner flank after local penetration', leading to 'a menacing move against his rear communications':[46]

> The key to success thus lies in rapidity of leverage, progressively extended deeper – in demoralizing the opposition by creating successive flank threats quicker than the enemy can meet them, so that his resistance as a whole or in parts, is loosened by the fear of being cut off.

Advancing on a wide front and making use of all available roads and tracks, the armoured forces should feel for gaps in the enemy's front and penetrate through them to create 'internal flanks'. 'In conjunction with this method there would seem to be promise in a wider application to the strategic advance of the method devised just after the War for infantry attack and christened the "expanding torrent".'[47] Opportunism ought to be turned into a system, by which initial successes are exploited and deepened. 'For mobile operations the risks of pushing too far and of committing reserves prematurely are minor compared with the cumulative risks of delay.'[48]

This was an astounding vision of things to come. But before going any further, there is another basic question to clarify: to what extent was Liddell Hart's theory of long-range strategic armoured operations uniquely his own? After all, it barely needs re-emphasizing that the development of the idea and practice of armoured warfare was a collective venture, worked for mainly within the army by a group of dedicated activists. Apart from Fuller and Liddell Hart, the accepted short list of the principal armour pioneers during the interwar period includes Giffard le Q. Martel, George Lindsay, Charles Broad, Percy Hobart, and Frederick 'Tim' Pile. Between these activists there was continuous interaction and exchange of views, from which Liddell Hart benefited as much as he contributed. By the mid-1920s all of them, following Fuller's ideas at the end and immediately after the First World War, in fact regarded independent, wide-ranging strategic moves as a field in which much of the potential of mechanized forces lay. And still, it was Liddell Hart's distinctive emphasis on the superiority of the strategic over the tactical that accounts for the definite lead which he held from the late 1920s onward in advocating the use of armoured forces for long-range, deep strategic penetrations.

We have earlier seen the way Liddell Hart distinguished in his *Memoirs* between what he regarded as Fuller's advocacy of *deep tactical* armoured penetration and his own views in favour of *deep strategic* penetration. In the wake of the German exploits during the Second World War he repeatedly emphasized this difference.[49] Significantly, however, Liddell Hart's distinction between Fuller's ideas and his own dates *not* from after the Second World War, when he could benefit from hindsight, but from *before* that war. He had formulated it in an unpublished critique he had written after reading Fuller's *Lectures on FSR III* (1932). In this remarkable document one reads:

> there is rather too much emphasis on the mechanism of tactics and not enough on the art, or on strategy ... [Fuller] concentrates too much on the old idea of 'battle' and does not point out how the strategic use of armoured forces may produce the opponent's downfall without a serious battle.
>
> While he deals at length with tactical penetration by tank forces, and in a masterly way, he does not consider the idea of a real *strategic penetration* – a stroke quick and deep, to cut the enemy's communications far back, where their main arteries can be severed....
>
> He adheres to the view he expressed in his book on 'Grant' – that a mobile force should be directed 'close to the rear' of the opposing army, instead of far in its rear – a stroke which may be more hazardous, but can be much more decisive, if it thoroughly severs the main arteries of supply....

He does not seem to have advanced beyond his 'Plan 1919' – a far reaching conception for that date, but not sufficiently long-range in the light of current possibilities. He pictures the mechanized army pushing forward in a series of limited bounds, long as tactical bounds, but too short for quickly decisive results.

Liddell Hart further argued that Fuller neglected the strategic pursuit and exaggerated the need for a strong 'tactical base' for the armoured force, a tendency which might deter commanders from venturing deep penetrations. He also pointed out that Fuller emphasized the need for close aerial cooperation with the tanks for reconnaissance, but not for fire-support.[50] This was despite the fact that the latter had already been practised both in the Battle of Amiens and in the Experimental Mechanized Force's manoeuvres.

Mearsheimer's erroneous claim that Liddell Hart did not advocate deep strategic penetration before the Second World War has obliged him to argue that Liddell Hart's critique of Fuller's *Lectures on FSR III*, the only evidence he has come across which could refute his claim, was in fact a fake, written after the Second World War.[51] However, in view of what we have seen regarding Liddell Hart's real positions, this allegation loses its ground. Even supposing the document were a fake, the fact remains that Liddell Hart's preoccupation, whole line of reasoning, and printed opinions in the early 1930s tally exactly with the views and themes expressed in his critique of Fuller's *Lectures on FSR III*.

Another, more significant, question is whether Liddell Hart's description of Fuller's positions was accurate and fair – generous it certainly was not. In later years Fuller himself pointed out to Liddell Hart that in his 'Plan 1919' he referred to 'strategic' as well as to 'tactical paralysis'.[52] All the same, if the semantics of what exactly constitutes 'strategic' is set aside, Liddell Hart was right in arguing that the 'Plan 1919' model – if only because of the limitations of the tanks then available or foreseen for the near future – envisaged an attack on the enemy's divisional, corps and army headquarters rather than long-range drives, many tens and even hundreds of miles deep, against the enemy's vital communications. Later, in the early 1920s, on the basis of Martel's seminal notions, Fuller developed his vision of mechanized land fleets, conducting large-scale operations across the country. As we have seen before, this vision decisively influenced the young Liddell Hart and the other advocates of mechanization. Here the scale of the movements envisaged was undoubtedly 'strategic'. Yet Liddell

Hart certainly had a point in the sense that Fuller's ideas ranged between the fairly concrete model of 'Plan 1919' and the futuristic vision of tank battle-fleets cruising the country, with the latter more sweeping model never assuming a more realistic down-to-earth form. In the late 1920s and during the 1930s both Fuller and Liddell Hart developed considerably, and dramatically widened their spheres of interest. Fuller, who moved on to investigate the causes and universal history of war, patently confessed that he had lost interest in the army and in mechanization. Senior officers in the Royal Tank Corps found him uncommunicative and somewhat out of touch.[53] His *Lectures on FSR III* (1932), admirable as it was, was little more than a formal exposition of the ideas which he had advanced in *The Reformation of War* (1923) and had repeated in *On Future Warfare* (1928). On the other hand, Liddell Hart's continuing and intimate involvement with the development of the British armoured force, coupled as it was with his overarching philosophy which promoted strategy over tactics, resulted in his developing of a sequence of remarkably acute and prophetic doctrine notions concerning the strategic use of armoured forces.

To be sure, some of his ideas proved untenable. On the Mongol and Sherman models he relentlessly preached logistic self-sufficiency, envisioning a streamlined armoured force, carrying only the bare necessities, living off the country-side, and aided in critical moments by the delivery of essential supplies from the air. Greatly exaggerating the ability of a mechanized force to exploit local resources, he believed that its logistic tail could be cut down to the minimum, allowing the force maximum freedom of operation.[54] In addition, it has been correctly pointed out that Liddell Hart was very dependent on the technical expertise of the soldiers and 'practical men'. For example, he warmly supported Martel's private project of a one-man tank, developed in the late 1920s as a modern substitute for mounted infantry, and needed Charles Broad to tell him that this was a wasteful and unpractical idea.[55]

This brings us to the senior officers of the Royal Tank Corps (RTC). What were their views in respect to deep strategic operations? The two men who exercised the greatest direct, day-to-day, influence on the evolution of the armoured force and its doctrine between 1923 and 1931 were George Lindsay and Charles Broad. The former became chief instructor of the Royal Tank Corps' Central Schools upon the establishment of the corps in 1923. In 1925 he became the inspector of the corps, a position he held until 1929. In September 1934, in the wake of Hobart's August manoeuvres, he was to command the first improvised Mobile Division during its trials. By 1925 Lindsay was fairly conscious of the possibilities of the deep, strategic use of armour. A first example of this can be seen in his correspondence in July of that year with Alan Brooke, then instructor at the Staff College at Camberley. Against Brooke's rather conservative view of the employment of tanks, he sketched out

> his picture of a future offensive battle, comprising three phases. First would come the assault of the enemy's main positions, carried out by tanks which would be 'assisted by all available fire-power and closely supported by infantry.' Second would be a tank pursuit to complete the tactical defeat of the defending forces, and 'to break up Command and Communications behind the captured positions'.... Third would come the strategic exploitation by a 'homogeneous Mechanicalized Force embracing the characteristics of all arms and accompanied by a large force of aircraft'.[56]

In his lectures at that time Lindsay quoted from Liddell Hart's essay on Mongol warfare. He sent his lectures to Hobart, then instructor at the Staff College in Quetta, India, and a new recruit to the RTC, and received the following response:

> I see you've been struck with the achievements of the Mongols.... Well – is it certain that the 'Mongolian' idea is dead? Extreme mobility – go for nerve centres. Live on the country. You'll only need petrol, oil and very little food (personnel comparatively small), all of which are endemic in any (even semi-civilized) country these days. You see – and (iron ration) supply by air. Why limit ourselves to 3,000–4,000 yards advance? The distance gunners can reach without moving.... Given (a) efficient, fast tanks with good means of control; (b) 'accompanying artillery' (i.e. The Royal Tank Artillery, designed for the support of tanks just as the R.H.A. was for the support of Cav.); (c) suitable air force. Why piddle about with porridge making of the Third-Ypres type? When one is possessed of modern weapon one shoots a tiger (or anything else) in the brain, heart, or spine.[57]

Lindsay replied as follows:

> The Mongol idea of extreme mobility, combined with great fire-power, is not dead, but lives. It is the line we must develop our

modern Mechanical Force. Yes, go for nerve-centres, and make the existence of the enemy field army impossible. Why fight for positions? If centres of command and supply, and communications, are overcome by the Mobile Force, the enemy cannot remain in their positions. Therefore why be obsessed with the idea of the necessity of fighting for them?

Lindsay went on to recommend to Hobart Liddell Hart's *Paris*, which he described as giving 'much food for thought'.[58]

But, of course, as everybody understood very well, the realization of all far-reaching visions depended on such practical matters specified in Hobart's letter: efficient fast tanks (now becoming available in the shape of the Vickers Medium Tank), adequate support and, most essentially, good means of control. 'Until we have the means of commanding and controlling tanks on the move, we cannot be a formation or force', wrote Hobart. 'Control of tanks', replied Lindsay, 'is a thing that we are working on hard now, but as yet we have not arrived at a solution, although we feel we are progressing.'[59] It was primarily these vital and complicated practical matters that preoccupied soldiers.[60] Charles Broad's work for the armoured force demonstrates this clearly. After serving under Lindsay, he succeeded him at the head of the RTC Central Schools in 1925. In 1927–31 he was in charge of SD2 in the General Staff, responsible for planning organization for war. When appointed to command the armoured brigade in the 1931 manoeuvres, he chose to concentrate on trying out a central system of radio control, on establishing the tank units' battle drill, and on regulating their tactics on the basis of flexible turning manoeuvres which he described as 'indirect approach'. The sensible nature of his decision was recognized by all, for clearly the armoured force had to learn to walk before it could run.[61]

Two years earlier, Broad was entrusted with the formulation of the pioneering official War Office manual *Mechanized and Armoured Formations* (1929), colloquially known because of the colour of its cover as the 'Purple Primer'. The booklet was reissued in a revised form as *Modern Formations* in 1931. It presented in a clear, persuasive and palatable manner the historical necessity of mechanization, the future vision of a progressively mechanized army and the doctrines of the armour advocates, including Liddell Hart. Here, too, however, Broad did not include long-range strategic operations.[62] Liddell Hart remarked that he was particularly well fitted to co-ordinate and crystallize the outpouring of new ideas that had spurted from several springs during the post-war years. His name most aptly typified his outlook – strongly progressive yet instinctively keeping a balance between the 'High' and 'Low' schools of military thought and theology.[63]

But then, the leading men of the Royal Tank Corps were understandably careful not to antagonize the system within which they were operating. As Liddell Hart fully recognized, Broad's non-provocative character and Lindsay's genial and sympathetic personality were major assets for the corps in the dealings within the army. They sharply contrasted with the abrasive personalities and uncompromising attitudes of Fuller and Hobart, which were to drive both of them out of any position of influence.

All this goes to explain why Liddell Hart, who for good or for ill was unencumbered by the priorities, practical considerations, essential technicalities, and day-to-day constraints which shaped the activities of the armour advocates within the army, was able to freely develop his already dominating strategic bias into a distinctive, far-reaching and prophetic conception of armoured warfare.

ii. Combating 'Blitzkrieg'

So during the 1920s and 1930s, in Fuller's footsteps, Liddell Hart developed the ideas that as employed by the Germans in 1939–41 would win them a string of brilliant victories. More about that in the next chapter. However, toward the middle of the 1930s Liddell Hart began to argue – and would become ever more insistent about this as the war was approaching – that great armoured breakthroughs were growing ever less likely to work owing to the increasing strength of the defence. This new note undoubtedly signified a major shift in his thought.

As Mearsheimer has rightly pointed out, this shift was intimately related to Liddell Hart's increasing preoccupation in the 1930s with policy and grand strategy.[64] In 1931–32, consulted by the British government regarding the position to be adopted in the coming Disarmament Conference in Geneva, he developed the scheme of 'qualitative disarmament', as opposed to the 'quantitative' approach around whose implementation the contentions between France and Germany in particular revolved. He thought that the best way to bypass the differences in the national points of view and deter aggression was to abolish 'offensive weapons', such as the heavy tank (above 5, 8 or 10 tons) and heavy gun (above 4-inch calibre), which had been developed as 'tin-openers' to overcome defensive lines and military stalemate. The new development in his thought was not easy for Liddell Hart because, as he admitted, it went against all that he had struggled for precisely to overcome defensive lines and military stalemate, chiefly by the use of the tank. But, as he pointed out, this had to be sacrificed for the 'wider view' of deterring aggression. 'There is a higher point of view than the general's – that of a statesman', he replied to Fuller's scathing criticism; 'Prevention is better than cure – and once war has begun, any cure is a highly uncertain one.' Furthermore, his reflections on the 'British way in warfare' the year before had already taught Liddell Hart that Britain in particular, with her 'preservative policy, insular position, limited resources, and inherent slowness in preparing for war', had little to gain from lightning land campaigns.[65]

As Liddell Hart was one of the earliest to recognize, Britain had developed into a modern, liberal-democratic, capitalist-consumerist and satisfied great power. As long as her interests were not directly threatened by major aggression, she felt she had nothing to gain from, and could no longer see herself voluntarily embroiled in, a total great-power war, entailing a massive loss of life and wealth. Thus, her strategic posture – foreshadowing that of the West as a whole later on – was fundamentally defensive, and her favourite strategic means were deterrence, containment, and economic coercion.[66]

Additional factors contributing to Liddell Hart's new trend of thought came from other directions. By 1931 he had completed *Foch*, in which he had delved into the problematic development of military ideas between 1871 and 1914. Having in addition dealt with the American Civil War in *Sherman*, he became very conscious that the face of future war had all too often been reflected in earlier wars, but had been radically misinterpreted because of wishful thinking and lack of intellectual courage to face reality. In many of its central salients 1914 continued the last phase of the American Civil War (1861–65), the Franco-Prussian War (1870–71), the South African War (1899–1902), and the Russian-Japanese War (1904–5).[67] In this respect, as in others, Liddell Hart grew more cautious with reflection, and his youthful enthusiasm was tempered. Now, with even greater attentiveness than before, he would always keep one eye on the First World War. In fact, many of the ideas he was advocating throughout the interwar period, such as the use of low-flying aircraft for close support and the execution of attacks under the cover of darkness and smoke, were simply derived from the experience of the successful offensives of 1918, particularly the Battle of Amiens.

At first, in 1933–35, Liddell Hart argued that, since the armies of the great powers retained their traditional character, being composed predominantly of infantry masses, the stalemate of trench warfare was most likely to recur in war. Under these conditions air power would only add to the paralysis of movement on the battlefield, unless really strong air forces were created. Armoured forces, operating deep in the enemy's rear, have the best chances of success, but they barely exist at the present. By contrast, motorized (lorry-mounted) formations, beginning to appear in all armies, would again only strengthen the defender by enabling him to rush machine-gun troops to threatened sectors of his front and block enemy advances. The best use of these forces in the offensive would be in combining the threatening strategic attack, or leap forward, with the tactical defence when the enemy is obliged to move out to check the advance. This was to be Sherman's 'baited offensive' revived. In sum, however, the defence retained, if not increased, its superiority, leaving little prospect for successful aggression.[68]

From 1935 on, as rearmament began in earnest and armoured divisions were increasingly being formed in all the major European armies, a new stage began. Would these new divisions break the stalemate, as Fuller, Liddell Hart and the other armour enthusiasts had believed in the 1920s? By the second half of the 1930s both Fuller and Liddell Hart had grown sceptical about it, and, as always, it had been Fuller who had led the way. From the late 1920s he had been developing his concept of the dialectic and spiralling evolution of the offensive and defensive means of war, which in his view had always inaugurated new eras in military history. He had been giving ever growing weight to the anti-tank gun and mine as the tank's equals. These would be used within a new system of defence in depth, in which the tank itself, concentrated in reserve for the counter-offensive, would play a major role.[69] Liddell Hart, always highly attentive to whatever Fuller was saying, picked up and elaborated on these ideas (indeed, pushed them to the extreme). In late 1935, discussing the British army's decision to create the Mobile Division which he desired so deeply, he wrote:

> It is setting expectations high to count on the programme of modernization to bridge the gulf that now separates armies from

their desire for successful attack. My own view is that these potential developments in offensive power are far exceeded by the actual growth, largely unrecognized, of defensive power.... Not only fire, but the means of obstruction and of demolition, may now be moved more swiftly to any threatened spot to thwart a hostile concentration of force.

Liddell Hart was no longer referring, as before, to old-style armies and to the old methods of defence and attack but specifically to the modern ones.[70]

He now increasingly used the very same arguments against overly optimistic expectations of tanks and of tank forces which he had rejected outright in the 1920s. It was as if he was paraphrasing the radicals' most thoughtful critic, Victor Germains; indeed he probably was. Only a couple of striking instances will be quoted here:

It should not be forgotten that the extraordinary successes gained in the World War by British and French tanks at Cambrai, Soissons, Amiens, were nothing else but surprises under conditions that would not occur again. They were gained (and they could only be gained) against a defence practically non-existent, impoverished with the most primitive of means, and completely inexperienced; and they could be expanded into decisive action only because the tank (at that time) was shrouded in the veil of the 'tank terror'.

It is true that tanks have been improved and increased, but anti-tank weapons have made still more rapid progress – and, being cheaper, can be multiplied faster.[71]

It was a decade earlier that Liddell Hart had mocked the claim that the development of the anti-tank gun would neutralize the tank, emphasizing the tank's superior mobility and employment in overwhelming concentrations in selected sectors of the front.[72]

In his acute analyses of the strategic lessons of the Spanish Civil War, Liddell Hart highlighted evidence which supported his view that 'the defence is paramount at present' and most likely to create stalemates. It is true that, while the performance of mechanized troops in Spain was widely regarded at the time as falling short of the radical expectations pinned upon them, he at first pointed out correctly that these troops were mainly no more than tracked infantry which did not possess offensive tactical capability. He called attention to the fact that the tanks used were early light models which all armies were in the process of replacing with heavier ones, and that in many cases these tanks were employed in small packets and over unsuitable ground.[73] However, in time he also began to stress that the Spanish Civil War demonstrated that large-scale tank breakthroughs were already a thing of the past.[74] It might be noted that not only 'conservative' general staffs were drawing similar conclusions at the time. In the Soviet Union, for example, citing the evidence from Spain and extensively quoting from Liddell Hart, none other than Marshal Mikhael Tukhachevsky wrote in 1937: 'In modern war the strength of the defence is steadily growing.... The advantage of defensive weapons lie in their ease of use and their large number.'[75]

As mentioned earlier, the change in Liddell Hart's views was heavily influenced by, and was subordinated to, his 'wider view' concerning Britain's and the West's favoured policy and grand strategy. If the defensive was gaining the ascendency and lightning mechanized coups were unlikely to succeed, the international status quo could be maintained more easily and cheaply. In late 1937, as British strategic policy was being decided upon, Liddell Hart wrote in his programmatic 'Defence or Attack' articles:

> So great is the power of the defensive nowadays that a small reinforcement may suffice to establish a deadlock ... comparatively slight provisions of up-to-date material – such as aircraft, anti-aircraft, artillery, and machine-guns – would have sufficed to make permanent and general the temporary and local stalemates which the aggressor repeatedly suffered.[76]

If things were really so, then Germany could be easily deterred or ringed by the powers and starved to submission, while the Allies would be foolish to invest enormous efforts and incur terrific losses in futile First World War style offensives. The ideas that Britain need not send an expeditionary force to the Continent (or send at most a small mechanized force); that France, in collaboration with her East European allies and particularly with the Soviet Union, could hold its own against Germany; but that no major offensive against Germany in the west was possible even if France were reinforced by the British – were all closely interdependent and largely based upon the power of the defence.[77] Thus, the more Liddell Hart convinced himself in this strategic formula, the more extreme he became in advocating the superiority of defence and in doing everything he could to eradicate the idea of a successful offensive.[78] His motivated bias regarding the strength of tactical and operational defence was getting ever stronger during the crisis years before the war. From 1937 he was an unofficial but highly influential adviser to the Secretary of State for War, Lesley Hore-Belisha, and was able push his ideas through.

The Chief of the Imperial General Staff Field Marshal Sir Cyril Deverell and the Director of Military Operations and Intelligence Major-General R.H. Haining tried to convince Liddell Hart that he was exaggerating. 'Haining also suggested that in my view of the superiority of the defence, I was relying too much on the experience of the last war. He remarked – "History never repeats itself"' – a view which Liddell Hart rejected.[79] When in late 1937 Deverell returned deeply impressed by the German army's manoeuvres, in which Panzer forces were employed for the first time on a large scale, his fate was sealed. 'He had come back from the German manoeuvres with the report that the French could not stand against them, that the Maginot line would not hold, and that the offensive would succeed.'[80] The stupidity of the man became so obviously dangerous in the eyes of Liddell Hart and Hore-Belisha that they decided to get rid of him. After a careful preparation of the political ground they acted swiftly. On 30 November the Cabinet authorized the removal of Deverell and of his deputy Knox, as well as a thorough purge of the Army Council. Lord Gort, Hore-Belisha's military secretary, who was on friendly relations with Liddell Hart, was pushed upwards to become the new CIGS. In December the memorandum 'On the Role of the Army' which Liddell Hart had prepared for Hore-Belisha was approved by the Cabinet.[81] British limited liability to the Continent became official policy. The revolution was complete. To use an analogy which Liddell Hart would have appreciated, it was a repetition in reverse of the famous incident of 1911 within the French high command: the head of the army, who foresaw the outline of the German attack in the approaching war, was removed by the civilian minister of war, supported by the 'Young Turks' in the army who had little faith in their chief. While in France this affair had been largely caused by, and had led to the victory of, the spirit of the *offensive à l'outrance*, in Britain it was prompted by what one of his contemporaries dubbed Liddell Hart's doctrine of the *défense à outrance*.[82]

During these years the fear that the French might take the offensive and drag the British along with them and into a massive continental commitment was paramount in Liddell Hart's mind. This was one of the reasons he preferred the dispatch to France of a few British armoured divisions rather than a traditional infantry army, which he believed would more easily and unaccountably be drawn into such offensives.[83] As the war approached, he grew increasingly more alarmed about this, insisting that only the offensive could lose the war for the Allies. After the defection of the Soviet Union and the outbreak of the war, the Allies were indeed incapable of attacking in the west and their military high commands recognized this very well and acted accordingly during the period known as the 'Phoney War'. But every rumour from General Headquarters inflamed Liddell Hart's suspicions that offensive schemes were being entertained.[84] Campaigning against any such venture, he found some reassurance in what he had learnt about the strategic positions of the French and British chiefs of staffs, Generals Maurice Gamelin and Edmund Ironside respectively, and about the former he repeatedly wrote in very favourable terms.[85]

In May–June 1940, within six weeks, the Low Countries and France fell before a German lightning campaign. Liddell Hart was as surprised as anybody. As his biographers have already revealed, contrary to what he would claim later on he had not foreseen even the possibility of a German victory. Quite the reverse, for years he had been insisting that France had been virtually secure from a German attack. His claim that the strength of modern defence had been paramount and had been continuing to grow was revealed to be fallacious. As Mearsheimer has shown in considerable detail, in later years Liddell Hart would do his utmost to eradicate this central and unhappy idea of his from historical memory. His *Memoirs* barely mention it. In his meeting with Daladier on 28–29 April 1938 Chamberlain justified the British policy of limited liability to the Continent by claiming that the power of the defensive in warfare had increased with modern methods and modern weapons; forms of attack previously thought of as irresistible, he argued, could now be met with a sufficiently organized defence. The official British historian who cites this wonders where Chamberlain found the inspiration for these views. But the answer to this, given the wording as well as the content of Chamberlain's argument, should not be too difficult to find.[86] Responsibility for the collapse of France could at least partly be laid at Liddell Hart's door. Consequently, his prestige suffered heavily and justly. Apart from anything else, he was made to look silly.[87]

It must have been an awful feeling for Liddell Hart, and his first apologetic efforts in his early war-time books to explain France 1940 – and the later 'Blitzkrieg' victories – often read rather pathetically.[88] He argued, for example, that he had been obliged to conceal his real views about the Allies' weakness in order not to assist the enemy and that he had developed his preference for the defensive before the war because he had known that the Allies possessed no real offensive weapon in the form of large mechanized forces. In truth, however, Liddell Hart favoured a defensive posture for the West predominantly because of what he regarded to be its ultimate political aims and in order to deter and limit war; only then did he increasingly convince himself that the defensive was tactically and operationally becoming ever stronger. Also, while Liddell Hart did claim (justly) that Britain lacked armoured forces suited for the offensive, this was mainly a contributing factor to his argument.[89] He did not believe the offensive would work for the Germans either.

Despite his continued criticism of many aspects of the mechanization of the British army, Liddell Hart in fact was generally much encouraged by the process finally set in motion in the British and French armies as they rearmed in the late 1930s. In view of that development he did not even strongly object to the mechanization of the cavalry, adopted in both Britain and France (and Germany) alongside the expansion of the armour corps. More surprisingly, during that period he also did not take a stand against the design and acquisition of special 'infantry tanks', the policy adopted by both the French and British armies.[90] He was encouraged by the growth in the number of French mobile formations and by the quality of their planned tank models; and this was partly, but not wholly, due to his desire to create a favourable impression of the French ability to confront the Germans without the support of a substantial British army. Mostly through Hobart, Liddell Hart was fully informed of the British intelligence reports which throughout the period portrayed a fairly good picture of the number, structure, strength, and doctrine of the main antagonists' tank formations. Before the war he accurately informed his readers that while the Germans possessed more armoured divisions than the French, the French had more and heavier tanks with their infantry.[91] The belief that by the 1940 campaign the Germans had managed to achieve overwhelming numerical superiority in tanks over the Allies was widely held just before and in the immediate aftermath of the German victory, and Liddell Hart used it to excuse himself in his wartime writings. But by the end of the war it became clear that the earlier estimates had been all too accurate and that it was in fact the Allies who held the superiority in tank numbers in May 1940, as well as enjoying rough parity in tank quality.[92]

So we turn back to tank doctrine. After 1940 Liddell Hart stressed that the Germans had applied the doctrine of armoured warfare which Fuller, himself and the other British armour pioneers had evolved from the 1920s. As we shall see, this was quite true. However, was not this fact much depreciated by Liddell Hart's loss of faith in the late 1930s in sweeping armoured offensives? Here, too, the answer is much more complex, and intriguing, than recent critics of Liddell Hart have allowed.

In the first place, it ought to be made clear that Liddell Hart's advocacy of the strength of defence by no means involved a withdrawal from the idea of armoured warfare. The battlefield and the sort of defence he foresaw before the war was thoroughly modern. It was dominated by mobile mechanized forces working closely with aircraft, but also by the anti-tank gun and other anti-tank means which would be engaged in a constant struggle for supremacy with the tank.[93] So long as they survived, traditional foot and horse-drawn troops would be relegated to a secondary and subsidiary role, except on special ground. The defence itself would take the form of mobile defence in depth, in which armoured and mechanized divisions, stationed in the defender's rear, would counter-strike to check and destroy large-scale penetrations by the enemy's mechanized formations.

A prevailing impression regarding the German 'Blitzkrieg method' is that it came as an almost total surprise to the Allies in the early war years. This was not at all the case. The skill of the Germans in carrying out 'Blitzkrieg' and its revolutionary successes certainly came as a surprise to the Allies – and to the Germans as well. But throughout the late 1930s the Allies' intelligence services and the Allied army commands in general had possessed a good picture not only of the strength and composition of the Panzer troops but also of their doctrine and intended method of employment. The old French fear of a German *attaque brusquée*, now to be carried out with armoured and mechanized divisions which without prior warning would overrun the French defensive lines, penetrate deep into the country and disrupt the French mobilization, was paramount in the Allies' strategic considerations and widely discussed.[94] Gort's comment to Liddell Hart was remarkably prophetic but not entirely uncommon:

> May it not be possible for Panzer divisions and concentrated air forces to effect a breach and this attack can take place with little previous warning. If by rapidity, deception and surprise it is possible to make a bridgehead then the war will pass into open country

once more. I feel novelty lies in some such direction as this as Belgium is hackneyed.[95]

To this and to Deverell's similar suggestion in a conversation with Liddell Hart the latter replied that the chances for such breakthroughs were doubtful and that modern and mobile defence, integrating armoured forces for counter-offensives, was likely to prove more effective.[96]

We have already seen how in the years 1935–37, far from deserting his earlier interest in armoured warfare, Liddell Hart himself developed the doctrine of large-scale armoured breakthroughs, which remarkably anticipated the outline of future 'Blitzkrieg'.[97] He foresaw the prospects of such offensives amazingly, but so did he also foresee their limitations. Time and again during those years he concluded his scheme of how deep armoured breakthroughs might be achieved with the following observations:

> Unless the defender signified his immediate surrender ... it would be necessary to follow up the strokes [of the armoured forces] with reinforcements and occupying forces. Here would lie the invader's hardest problem.... It is conceivable that an attacker by extraordinary foresight, by gauging the trend of developments exactly, and by perfectly calculated measures to diminish his own vulnerability while maintaining his strength, might succeed in producing the internal collapse of his adversary without courting his own – but such foresight has never been shown by any makers of war.[98]

> There is little doubt that the new mechanized divisions which the European armies now possess will be used in the first hours of war with the aim of penetrating the enemy's frontier and opening the way for the subsequent general advance.... But there is reason to doubt whether this mechanized spearhead will produce the decisive advantage which is sought. The chances are against this, unless the enemy is not only taken unaware but is himself unmechanized.

The main problem would be deliberate obstruction and counter-attacks by mechanized forces brought forward against the threat.[99]

Finally, in Liddell Hart's 'Defence and Attack' series, after outlining his method for deep strategic penetration:

> The general deduction that the defensive has a great and growing superiority does not, of course, imply that the offensive can never

succeed. It is likely to succeed, as already noted, in a campaign where the defender has no effective counter-weapons to nullify such offensive instruments such as aircraft and tanks. It may possibly succeed against an opponent of similar equipment if the attacker displays a great superiority of art, and thereby produces a great local superiority of fire and psychological threat.[100]

Everyone familiar with the theme of 'the rise and fall of Blitzkrieg' during the Second World War cannot fail to be impressed by these insights. For Liddell Hart France 1940 was an accident, albeit a terrible and fateful one. During the second half of the 1930s he consistently emphasized the role of armoured formations which would be kept in the rear for counter-attacks against enemy armoured penetrations within a modern system of mobile defence in depth.[101] For Liddell Hart it was the story of the 'expanding torrent' versus the 'contracting funnel' of the later stage and immediate aftermath of the First World War all over again, only by means of mechanized rather than infantry forces and, consequently, on a wider scale and much quicker pace. It was again the system of modern defence in depth to be developed against an initially successful method of modern attack in depth, as had been the case with the German 'infiltration tactics' of 1917–18. While valuing the Maginot line, Liddell Hart pointed out accurately that it was intended mainly as a covering and delaying line against a sudden German attack and would require strong mobile reserves behind it. This was precisely the role he persistently advocated for the British armoured formations in conjunction with the French mobile divisions.[102]

Indeed, as recent research has shown, this was also the role the French themselves envisaged in the second half of the 1930s for their new heavy armoured divisions (DCR), which were to be reinforced by a British armoured contribution and further supported by the French cavalry-type armoured divisions (DLM) and motorized infantry divisions. Contrary to lingering popular images, serious attention was given in France during those years to operational planning for mobile defence in depth. To be sure, French tank production was lagging, and the British armoured contribution failed to be ready in time for the Battle of France. Nevertheless, by the time of that battle, the French had been hastily creating their third and beginning to create their fourth DCR (*Division Cuirassée de Réserve*), which as their title indicate, were specifically intended for the counter-offensive role against the Panzer divisions and destined for deployment as a strong mobile reserve in the area of Laon, Rheims, and Châlons-sur-Marne, at the centre of the French line. While these heavy formations were still inexperienced and suffered from many deficiencies, the three DLMs, although also inferior to the all-round combat concept of the German Panzer divisions, were well trained and incorporated the new and excellent SOMUA medium tanks. And the seven French motorized divisions in fact slightly outnumbered their German counterparts.[103] Although the doctrine of the French army during the interwar period negated the idea of a mobile battle of manoeuvre, the chances of these mobile formations to check German armoured penetrations were not altogether unfavourable, had not things turned out so badly for the Allies.

For the Allies collapse in the west in 1940 was not foretold but involved a strong element of chance. Until the beginning of 1940 the Germans planned a fairly conventional and limited advance into Holland and Belgium, spearheaded by their armoured and mechanized divisions. To this the Allies intended to respond by an advance into Belgium, led by their own mobile troops, either to the line of the River Scheldt (Plan E) or, more ambitiously, to the line of the River Dyle (Plan D). Both Liddell Hart and Fuller pointed out at the time that a campaign in the west would be an entirely different ball game than the one the Germans had experienced in Poland. Belgian and Dutch territory was cut by rivers and water channels, posing great difficulty for mechanized forces, and in addition the Germans would face modern equipped adversaries.[104] Senior German officers held the same view. In the opinion of Franz Halder, chief of the German general staff: 'Techniques of Polish campaign no recipe for the West. No good against a well-knit army.' According to General Ritter von Leeb, also rejecting the Polish comparison, 'the high value of the French army and its leadership must not be underrated and the equipment with armoured units and anti-tank weapons of the French and English armies must not be forgotten.'[105]

It was only during February–April 1940 that both sides altered their plans. The falling of the German attack plans into Allied hands when a German aircraft crash-landed in Belgium precipitated developments which had already been evolving before the incident. The Germans adopted Erich von Manstein's plan which switched their main offensive thrust, including most of their mobile divisions, southwards, to the Ardennes region. Almost simultaneously, the Allies, still expecting the main offensive to come from the north, adopted an even more ambitious version of the Dale plan, incorporating the so-called Breda extension. The plan envisaged a rapid deep advance into Holland by the Allies' extreme left wing, distracting the cream of the French mobile divisions (and the semi-mobile British Expeditionary Force) westward. Only after that advance would have been completed were these divisions planned to be withdrawn once more to the role of mobile reserve.[106] In view of the new German plans, the Allies' order of battle was thus taken disastrously out of balance. Not only were the Allies' best troops deployed in the wrong direction, but the Allies' mobile strategic reserve was left dangerously weak. Despite desperate efforts, this situation proved impossible to remedy when the full significance of the German breakthrough through the Ardennes became clear. When on 16 May, at the height of the crisis, Churchill arrived in France with the memory of the crisis of 1918 in mind and asked Gamelin where the Allies' strategic reserve was stationed, he was shocked to learn that there was practically none available.[107] Under these circumstances, the German mechanized forces were only haphazardly and sporadically opposed during their breakthrough and race to the Channel. The conditions which Liddell Hart had specified for the complete success of a 'Blitzkrieg' campaign, and had regarded as exceptional, were disastrously realized.

Thus in his efforts to excuse himself after 1940 Liddell Hart argued that the fall of France had not been inevitable but had been caused by extraordinary strategic blunders on the part of the Allies' high command. In the immediate aftermath of the defeat, he himself wavered on the exact line the Allies should have taken.[108] But on the main issue, the French total neglect of the Ardennes, which had been traditionally regarded as unsuitable for the operations of large formations,[109] Liddell Hart possessed a good personal record upon which to base his criticism. For after travelling through the Ardennes in 1928, he came to the conclusion that, contrary to Allied perceptions in 1918, this region was not unsuitable for the movement of large formations, a point he repeated in the following decade in his successive books on the First World War.[110] In May 1936, after the German occupation of the Rhine demilitarized zone and more than a year before Gort would suggest to him the possibility of a German armoured breakthrough in a sector different from the traditional Belgian route, Liddell Hart had a talk (which he recorded at the time) with Brigadier Ronald Adam and Colonel Bernard Paget:

> I remarked that there was still a danger interval before the new Belgian defence were completed, or those of the French along the

German frontier. I suggested that we ought not overlook the possibility that if the French took the offensive, the Germans while meeting them defensively, would launch a flank counter-stroke through Belgian Luxembourg with their 3 Mechanized divisions [then in existence; A.G.].

Paget said that the chances were that the Belgians would have sufficient time to man their fortifications, but Liddell Hart replied that the Germans might attack by surprise.[111]

These various observations, made in different contexts, do not of course imply that Liddell Hart in any way 'predicted' the route the Germans would choose in 1940. He did not. No one, including the Germans, did or could have. They simply demonstrate that Liddell Hart had been clearly and more than most aware of the passibility of the Ardennes to large formations, including modern mechanized ones; and it was largely on this awareness that the campaign in the west in 1940 hinged, and was lost. In 1939 Liddell Hart's carefully weighed survey of the salient features of the defence of the western front and of the various strategic options open to the antagonists was on the whole optimistic about the prospects of the defence in the Ardennes sector, assuming the right measures were adopted. The region, he wrote,

> might prove a strategic trap for an invader if he fails to cross the Meuse.... For the Belgians, the obvious plan of defence is to make sure of holding the Meuse moat, together with the Liège bridgehead beyond it, while utilizing the Ardennes as a spring-buffer to absorb the shock of any hostile advance which come through that way. The Ardennes offer such a series of fine defensive positions that it would be desirable to employ here sufficient forces to develop the full delaying power of this vast obstacle. It is difficult, however, for the Belgians to do so from their own resources without jeopardizing their main position on the Meuse. Moreover, they have to reckon with the possibility of having to meet danger from a new direction, where they are more vulnerable – on their Dutch flank.... The full development of the potentialities of the Ardennes as an obstacle thus depend on whether, and how soon, the limited Belgian forces here can be reinforced by those of a guarantor Power. During a recent tour ... it was revealing to find how immensely strong by nature were the series of positions – the gorge of the Semois, the heights north of Sedan, and the Meuse –

upon which the French might have stood [in 1914], yet which in the event they so swiftly abandoned.... If present-day Belgian strategy visualizes the Ardennes as the scene of a manoeuvre in withdrawal, not of a rigid resistance, in face of superior numbers, there is ample evidence of preparations designed to make any hostile progress a march in slow time, and to compel an enemy to make the most exhaustive efforts ... at many points ... a handful of machine-guns might hold up an army corps. It is clear that the scheme of defence is planned to make the most of these numerous possible Thermopylae.[112]

The concept in itself was impeccable and in step with the ideas Liddell Hart had been developing in the second half of the 1930s regarding flexible defence in depth. Lacking the benefit of hindsight it kept all the options open. Given the uncertainty regarding the direction of the German main offensive efforts, and especially the possibility of a German turning movement through Dutch territory, the Ardennes were viewed as a scene of a delaying manoeuvre on the Allies' part. Relying on the topographical features of that region, which made it the perfect shock-absorber, field fortifications, field forces, and wide-scale obstruction should be used to delay enemy columns long enough for the Allies to take up their main fortified line of defence along the heights overlooking the Meuse and deploy their mechanized reserves behind it. The attacking spearheads would then find themselves in an awkward position, experiencing logistic problems and having limited room for deployment and mutual support.

This assessment of the situation, made the year before the war, underpinned Liddell Hart's reactions when the campaign in the west was launched on 10 May 1940. On the 11th he noted that the German advance through Holland, upon which all eyes in the Western camp were fixed, had been expected, but also pointed out that it might be a diversion. Two days later, before the German advance through the Ardennes became publicly known and the centre of attention, his overall survey of the front again mentioned the Ardennes as a scene for delaying action. On the 15th, as the Ardennes offensive and the German crossing of the Meuse became known, Liddell Hart wrote that the attack had been expected, but now that the Germans had reached Sedan the situation had become serious. He maintained, however, that French armour was designed specifically to meet such a German breakthrough, and even on the 19th, when all was lost, argued that the danger must not be exaggerated, for the German armoured penetration would hopefully lose its momentum. Things were not as bad as they had been in 1914 or 1918. At the beginning of June Liddell Hart was still hoping for Allied counter-offensives which would stop the Germans as in 1918, and only on the 6th he finally resigned himself to the idea that the armour required for counter-attacking was simply not in place.[113]

Wholly concentrating on the Dutch and Flanders routes, the Allies' high command left the Ardennes covered by only thirteen, mostly second- and third-class divisions. These forces were not designed to, and were incapable of, pushing strong delaying forces into the Ardennes. When the German Army Group A, totalling forty-four divisions, including seven Panzer and three motorized, and massively supported by the Luftwaffe, rolled into the Ardennes, the French were only able to push in one horse cavalry division and several infantry battalions. Thus, even though the Belgian delaying forces performed quite effectively, especially on 10 May, the German mechanized spearheads encountered little opposition and no wide-scale obstruction. By the end of 13 May, the Germans began to cross the Meuse, which the weak French forces in the area again proved incapable of holding. Since the French high command was slow to realize what was happening, the battle by then was practically lost.[114]

So what does all this prove in respect to Liddell Hart's doctrines of armoured warfare? There is no doubt that his overriding concern during the 1930s to devise a limited strategic response to the Nazi challenge biased his judgement, most notably regarding the superiority of the defensive. He was all too eager to take new developments which were only beginning to take shape, such as the Allies' acquisition of tanks and anti-tank guns and creation of mobile formations, as if they were already a reality rather than an incomplete and greatly deficient process. As he wrote revealingly in a tortured brief reference to the matter in his *Memoirs*: 'In this urgent effort to press for the development of an effective defensive technique, and to convince military opinion of its value, I did not emphasize the qualifying factors as fully and frequently as I should have done.'[115] In addition, although the battlefield Liddell Hart foresaw was dominated by modern mobile forces rather than by the traditional arms of the First World War, he portrayed it all too frequently if not as static then at least as frozen in the operational sense as the battlefields of the Western Front in the previous war. On this he probably exaggerated, even in the long run. And yet, viewed from a more distant perspective, was he on the whole that wrong or mainly over-hasty?

As Liddell Hart would repeatedly point out for the rest of his life, by the second half of the Second World War all armies learned how to contend with armoured breakthroughs and developed the techniques and the means for blunting them. These, he would claim, were the techniques of mobile defence in depth which he had already suggested and advocated in the second half of the 1930s. By 1942, both in Russia and in North Africa, such techniques put an end to the spectacular spate of 'Blitzkrieg' successes. Thereafter, in Italy, Western Europe and the Eastern Front, the war again became a gigantic struggle of attrition. Offensive operational success was now achieved only under conditions of overwhelming superiority in *matériel*, the very conditions Liddell Hart had insisted would be required in his pre-war writings. More remarkably, Liddell Hart did not make this argument of self-justification retrospectively but in fact advanced it well before the event. In late 1940, after the dramatic fall of France and *prior* to the occurrence of even one instance of a successful defence in depth against mechanized forces, Liddell Hart wrote in *Dynamic Defence*, referring of course to himself:

> ... the knowledge gained in developing the new offensive technique led to the discovery of an effective counter-technique. But it had taken fully ten years to gain official acceptance for the former, and even then in a half-hearted way. So it was perhaps too much to expect that the antidote could have been approved and prepared in time, unless the war had been postponed until 1945!

He repeated his forecasts from the preceding years:

> While it is axiomatic that the attacker enjoys the advantage of the initiative, it may not carry him far save where he is met by slow-moving forces. The advantage is likely to be short-lived if the defender disposes of adequate mechanized forces. The advance of the attacker's armoured units through the defence, if they are in depth, is likely to be slower than the bringing up of the defender's armoured units along unobtrusive roads, or across country that they know. On arrival they can strike the attacker's armoured force at the moment when it is likely to be somewhat disorganized by its fighting advance.

This would be 'a reversed form of "soft spot" tactics', supplementing 'gradually contracting funnels' of defensive dispositions, in which 'the lanes would now be hedged with anti-tanks guns.'[116]

Public reputations are a volatile commodity, sensitive to wild market fluctuations. In hindsight the source of Liddell Hart's disgrace may be revealed in a different light. If one were to take a very favourable view of the development of his ideas, one could suggest that, rather than being – like the proverbial generals – always ready for the last war, he was consistently one war ahead in his thought: whereas in the 1920s he anticipated the triumph of 'Blitzkrieg' in 1939–42, in the second half of the 1930s he was looking ahead to its demise in 1942–45.

iii. *The all-arms armoured formation*

Liddell Hart's other major claim in his *Memoirs* for greater prescience than Fuller's concerned the use of infantry in close co-operation with the tanks within the armoured force, which Liddell Hart argued he had advocated whereas Fuller had rejected. This was a matter of great significance in the context of the post-Second World War debate, for the failures of the British armour in the early campaigns against Rommel in North Africa was largely attributed to what was termed its 'all-tank' conception, as opposed to the German 'all-arms' combination in the Panzer divisions. It should be noted, however, that here, too, Liddell Hart's criticism dated from before the Second World War, with his *Memoirs* essentially repeating the comments he had made in the early 1930s on *Fuller's Lectures on FSR III*.[117]

But again, how accurately did Liddell Hart present the differences between Fuller and himself on this subject? Critics have pointed out that Fuller had not in fact favoured an 'all-tank' army but rather maintained that other arms such as artillery and engineers would be mounted on tracked armoured vehicles, to which he had sometimes referred as types of tanks.[118] As was often the case in his *Memoirs* (he used a more accurate language in his critique of *Lectures on FSR III*), Liddell Hart did not miss an opportunity to misleadingly widen the gap between himself and his perceived contenders.[119] Noticeably, however, Fuller himself did not deny or try to refute Liddell Hart's claims when after the Second World War the latter confronted him with the differences in their positions on this subject during the inter-war years.[120]

Fuller's position from the early 1920s on derived from his all-encompassing vision of armies in the machine age. In the immediate postwar years, when he was still advancing programmes for gradual mechanization, he visualized a changing balance taking place between the infantry and tank components of the army. He maintained that in the end this would leave only small mechanized infantry units to support the tanks within a mechanized army, as opposed to the tanks supporting the mass of foot infantry in the armies of the time.[121] However, from 1922 on Fuller mainly projected deep into the future, and in his future army and future battlefield infantry would have only two functions. He divided ground into two main categories: open, designated 'tank area', and closed, 'infantry area'. In the latter, which encompassed forest, mountain and swamp land, infantry would continue to dominate, reorganized as light infantry. By contrast, in the main, 'tank country', apart from policing and occupation missions, infantry, though mounted on cross-country armoured vehicles and forming part of the mechanized army, would have only a very limited and totally defensive role to play. Protected by trenches, ramparts and mines, it would hold the tanks' mobile fortified bases and garrison strategic strongholds. Offensive warfare would be conducted solely by the tanks, aided by armoured pioneers and by mechanized, especially heavy siege, artillery.[122]

Now what were Liddell Hart's positions and development *vis-à-vis* Fuller's? As we have already seen, between 1922 and 1927 he was almost totally under Fuller's influence. In his last infantry articles (1922), written after he had converted to armour, in his RUSI essay on mechanization (1922) and derivative articles (1924), and in *Paris* (1925) he completely reproduced Fuller's picture of mechanized armies, dominated by the tanks and followed by heavy artillery and by mechanized infantry in the mobile bases. Consistently, however, he diverged from Fuller's vision on one point, cautiously expressed but *always* there. He wrote that, although infantry would be greatly reduced in number and significance, it would continue to exist within the mechanized battlefield, and in more than a defensive role. Its function would always be to dig the enemy out of its holes. For that purpose it would be mounted on cross-country armoured vehicles and accompany the tanks in close support, as 'land marines'.[123]

> To sum up our deductions – The land 'punch' of the future will be delivered by fleets of tanks, their communications maintained by cross-country and air vehicles.... These quick-moving and quick-hitting forces will advance by rapid bounds into the enemy country to strike at its vitals, establishing behind them, as they progress, a chain of fortified bases, garrisoned by heavy artillery and land marines – *late* infantry. A proportion of land marines might also be

carried in this tank fleet to be used as 'landing parties' to clear fortifications and hill defences under cover of the fire from the tank fleet.[124]

In the following years Liddell Hart continued to mention the need for foot infantry for hill and wooded country and for tank marines for 'mopping up' and for holding occupied ground behind the tanks, until replaced in the latter function by mounted machine guns.[125]

So there was a difference here, barely distinguishable at times, but certainly expressing a conscious divergence from Fuller's well-known position. The only snag is that this difference was much less relevant to the Second World War debate than Liddell Hart pretended. He had a special talent for framing a question in his own favour – and to his adversary's disadvantage. The point which he knowingly and cleverly blurred, was that the debate over the composition of the British armoured divisions during the Second World War was not between the views that he and Fuller respectively represented, but rather went against them both. For consistently throughout his life – during the interwar period, at the time of the Second World War and up until the 1960s – Liddell Hart advocated a wholly armoured division, very heavy in tanks, and containing only a small element of armoured infantry.

Ever since the inception of the Royal Tank Corps all the leading advocates of armour visualized the armoured formation as consisting solely of cross-country armoured vehicles. However, the Experimental Force created in 1927 included a battalion of 'motorized', rather than 'armoured' infantry, a development to which many of the armour activists, including Liddell Hart, objected on the grounds that lorry-mounted infantry lacked both the protection and the cross-country mobility to co-operate effectively with the tanks. Liddell Hart, for example, suggested that one company of armoured 'tank marines' was all the brigade needed.[126] The trials confirmed the armour activists in their view. Although in *Mechanized and Armoured Formations* (1929) and more extensively in its successor *Modern Formations* (1931) Broad found it politic to allow for the tank formations being supported by 'bused' infantry, the manual added somewhat inconsistently that 'these must be able to travel at the same pace as armoured fighting vehicles'.[127]

The question came to a head when the British army began to seriously consider the creation of a 'Mobile Division', a process which began in 1934, after the establishment of the Tank Brigade, and was not fully completed before the outbreak of the war. In the autumn of 1934 an improvised Mobile Division commanded by Lindsay was tried for the first time, with the Tank Brigade under Hobart co-operating with the newly mechanized 7th Infantry Brigade and other supporting units. Among the leading armour activists Lindsay in particular had always advocated a mixed, all-arms, structure for the armoured formations, even though he, too, envisaged a predominantly defensive role in the fortified base for the infantry.[128] In late 1933, in preparation for the next year's trial, he and Hobart, while agreeing on the use of the future armoured formation mainly for independent long-range operations, crystallized somewhat different conceptions regarding its shape and composition. Hobart saw it consisting mainly of the Tank Brigade, aided by a group of subsidiary supporting elements, whereas Lindsay proposed a larger and more balanced structure, consisting of the Tank Brigade, a motorized cavalry brigade (armoured cars and motorized machine-guns), a motorized infantry brigade, and supporting elements.[129] The 1934 trials of the Mobile Division were regarded as unsuccessful and resulted in Lindsay's departure to India and eventual retirement. Although this had little to do with his conception of the armoured division, the scene was now cleared of the only senior officer in the Royal Tank Corps who had always regarded this division as a more truly all-arms formation.

The issue of the composition of the Mobile Division became all the more complicated owing to the lack of cooperation, divisions and rivalries between the various arms and services. The Royal Air Force and the Royal Artillery, for example, failed to provide the machines and type of support the tank men requested for the armoured formations.[130] The army's decisions in 1935, in the first place, not to expand the Royal Tank Corps but instead to mechanize the cavalry, and, secondly, to equip the cavalry with light tanks rather than turn them into mechanized infantry, were other major influences on the shape of the evolving Mobile Division. There was also a serious intention to make the Mobile Division a mechanized cavalry formation, from which the Tank Brigade would be excluded. The division was thus to become a light force intended for reconnaissance, screening and raiding rather than a striking force for the main battle. As Hobart argued and Liddell Hart later told the CIGS Deverell, in this form it would be smashed in an encounter with German armoured divisions. Being now the power behind the throne as adviser to Hore-Belisha, Liddell Hart was instrumental in reversing the army's decision.[131]

All the same, the armour enthusiasts themselves were a major blocking force for the shaping of the Mobile Division as a more balanced all-arms team. In this respect, as in others, Hobart and Liddell Hart were basically at one. Liddell Hart believed that mixing armoured and unarmoured units in the division was not a good idea. Specifically regarding the infantry he wrote following the 1934 manoeuvres:

> A tank force may sometimes need men on foot to force river crossings for it, and also, when halted, to enable the crews to rest undisturbed by snipers and harassing parties. But to attach a whole embussed infantry brigade to it seems a mistake; it cramps its freedom of manoeuvre, and doubles the target. To carry a small number of 'tank marines', as one suggested years ago, still seems the better solution.[132]

The emphasis here was two-pronged, a point about which Liddell Hart was evasive and misleading in his later histories.[133] In September 1937, as the struggle over the composition of the Mobile Division reached its peak, Hobart suggested that a separate reconnaissance formation would be created, while the armoured formation itself would include one or two cavalry light-tank regiments, a tank brigade, and a 'holding group' of mounted rifles, engineers, and anti-tank, anti-aircraft and medium artillery.[134] A few months later Liddell Hart proposed to Hore-Belisha that instead of having two mechanized cavalry brigades and one tank brigade in the Mobile Division, it would consist of only two regiments of mechanized cavalry and of two tank brigades, thus sensibly reducing its tank establishment from 620 (mainly light) to 390 (mainly medium), while at the same time strengthening its punch. In Liddell Hart's view the units saved could be economically used to create a second mobile division. All the same, his proposed division still comprised only two infantry battalions in the 'support group', and he had doubts regarding the need for artillery.[135] A restructuring along these lines was carried out in 1939, with the infantry component of the renamed Armoured Division further reduced to only one battalion in its 'support group'.[136]

In summary, there were two problems with the armour enthusiasts' position, a position which they all – Liddell Hart included – had inherited from Fuller. In the first place, no country in the 1930s or 1940s had the resources and manufacturing capacity for fully providing the non-tank elements in its armoured formations with tracked armoured vehicles, desirable as this may have been in principle. The alternative was between having the non-tank elements in the armoured division 'motorized' rather than fully 'mechanized', or not having them at all. From the outset the Soviet armour pioneers accepted this fact of life without much difficulty and chose the first option, and even Guderian and the German creators of the Panzer arm, who had been decisively influenced by the British school, were obliged to do the same. More seriously, however, than the problem of 'motorization' versus 'mechanization', the British armour pioneers simply underestimated the quantity of infantry and artillery – in whatever form – required in the armoured formation. Experience during the Second World War was to show that 'tanks areas' and 'infantry areas', 'tanks jobs' and 'infantry jobs' were much more mixed than even Liddell Hart, who supported a small element of offensive armoured infantry in the armoured division, realized.

Surprisingly, however, the Second World War caused very little change in the pre-war positions and alignments on either side in Britain regarding the role and composition of the armoured formation. The initial shock caused by the German successes, particularly the overrunning of the Low Countries and France in 1940, prompted the army to plan the creation of nine armoured divisions, and a further expansion to almost double that number was envisaged.[137] However, the failures of the British armour in the early campaigns against the Germans in North Africa, especially its vulnerability to the German anti-tank guns, soon confirmed the army's high command in the view, most typically represented by the CIGS Alan Brooke, that the importance of the tank had been exaggerated and that it was, in any case, already past its peak. This view would later be reinforced by the campaigns in Italy and north-western Europe. During the later phase of the war the number of British armoured divisions was therefore reduced from the eleven actually created to five, and the composition of the armoured division was changed. In the spring of 1942, in imitation of the German Panzer divisions and in the light of the lessons derived from Operation Crusader, the number of tank brigades in the armoured divisions was reduced from two to one, with the division's tank establishment respectively reduced from some 320 to around 160. A full motorized infantry brigade (instead of the already increased number of two infantry battalions in the now discarded 'support group') was included in the division together with a mechanized artillery brigade. This was the form which the armoured division was to retain up until the end of the war. The American armoured forces underwent similar development.[138] The change did not, however, pass without opposition, which was again voiced mainly by Hobart inside, and Liddell Hart outside the army.

In the summer of 1941, in the wake of the great German successes, Liddell Hart argued that even the then existing type of armoured division included too many unarmoured elements, which also made it too large and cumbersome. Its roughly 2000 vehicles, he maintained, precluded logistic self-sufficiency and made it totally dependent on a huge logistic tail. He proposed that the number of tank brigades in a division be raised from two to three (implicitly, from roughly 320 to 480 tanks); that the motorized infantry battalion newly included in each tank brigade be removed; and that all motorized infantry and lorry- and tractor-drawn artillery, anti-tank and anti-aircraft guns be transferred to the corps level, together with much of what Liddell Hart regarded as excess transport. The armoured division he proposed was thus to be smaller than the existing one but composed almost entirely of tanks, supported by only a small number of self-propelled howitzers and wheeled reconnaissance units. On this occasion Liddell Hart did not even refer to armoured infantry and would mention them again only a few months later.[139]

When the re-organization of the armoured divisions took a diametrically opposite direction, Liddell Hart staunchly objected to the change in a series of memoranda.[140] He was kept well informed of the planned reform by Hobart, who in late 1940 had been returned by Churchill from a forced retirement and given command of an armoured division, only to find himself again isolated and at the centre of controversy. Holding to the same views that he and Liddell Hart had always advocated, he was at odds with Martel, the commander of the Royal Tank Corps, who supported the reform.[141] Writing to Liddell Hart in 1943, Martel argued that Liddell Hart was going too far with his 'all-armour' conception and that the armoured divisions ought to combine both armoured and unarmoured mobile units.[142] Liddell Hart, however, continued to claim relentlessly that a true armoured division had not yet been created and tested anywhere, and that those presently bearing that title, including the German Panzer divisions, were in fact 'inverted turtles', in which a small armoured spearhead led a large, cumbersome and vulnerable unarmoured body.[143] For the rest of his life – during the war, the 1950s and the 1960s – Liddell Hart did not change his views on the matter one bit, rejecting all prophecies that the tank's days were over and calling for the creation of small but tank-heavy armoured divisions, in which the infantry component would be decreased and all supporting elements would be given armoured protection and cross-country mobility.[144] In letters to Martel he drew up his defences against the 'all-tank' charge which was gaining currency in the later part and aftermath of the war, defining his own position as 'all-armour' and throwing on Fuller the derogatory 'all-tank' label.[145] Since Hobart, with whom he had collaborated so closely and who had always held the same opinions as himself, was also victimized by that label, Liddell Hart was careful in his postwar writings not to associate himself too closely with him. In this he succeeded remarkably, breaking loose from the 'all-tank' charge, but at the cost of diminishing his own credit for the 1934–37 manoeuvres.

As already mentioned, the misleading 'all-tank' label, which Liddell Hart did not create but which he used to his convenience, only served to blur the real issue, for no armour enthusiast anywhere during the interwar period had ever held an 'all-tank' conception, whereas most insisted on a cross-country and all-armoured, tank-heavy formula (in the case of Fuller and his disciples – an 'all-armour', no *offensive* infantry in 'tank areas'). Indeed, if Liddell Hart's views on the desired composition of the armoured division were contradicted by experience, much of his criticism was shared by Guderian well into the Second World War, and, what is more, with explicit reference to Liddell Hart's writings. When nominated Inspector General of Armoured Troops after Stalingrad one of Guderian's main objectives was to bring the tank strength of the Panzer division, depleted by low tank-production and the terrific losses sustained in the war on the Eastern Front back to its 1938 establishment of 400 tanks, even if that meant a reduction in the overall number of armoured divisions. To be battle-effective, he explained in a meeting with Hitler and senior staff officers on 9 March 1943, the Panzer division had to be very strong in tanks. To support his point he read out to Hitler and the attending officers a recently published article by Liddell Hart on the organization of armoured forces – past and present.[146] Guderian, Hobart, and Liddell Hart were in this respect practically at one.

2
British Influence and the Evolution of the Panzer Arm

Liddell Hart's reputation as one who decisively influenced the proponents of armoured warfare in Germany during the interwar period has recently been marred and thrown into question. It has been revealed that this reputation was largely self-propagated, and that to create it he actually exploited the plight in which the German generals were after the Second World War, unscrupulously manipulating their evidence for his own ends.[1] For several years after the war the German generals were detained as prisoners of war by the Allies, awaiting the decision on whether to put them on trial for war crimes. Liddell Hart made contact with a group of them who were held not far from his house in the Lake District. He interviewed them on their prewar and war experiences and soon developed further contacts with other senior German generals held in Germany. Their evidence served as the basis for his book *The Other Side of the Hill* (1948), or *The German Generals Talk*, as the American edition was called. Out of deepest conviction and best of motives, Liddell Hart became one of the leaders of an unpopular public campaign on the German generals' behalf. He argued relentlessly that they were no more than honourable and patriotic professional soldiers who had generally kept aloof from politics, had had an instinctive class and caste dislike for the Nazi regime, and had not been involved in Nazi atrocities. In *The Other Side of the Hill* he collaborated with the defeated and apologetic generals in developing this influential line of argument, which later historical research would increasingly qualify and reject. He denounced as unjust and vindictive the intention to prosecute the generals as war criminals, acted to improve their prison conditions, and tried to ease their discomfort by personally sending them parcels with small amenities such as food and tobacco. Only by going through his files can one get a true measure of the immense time and effort he invested in the matter over the years. Naturally, Liddell Hart's personal contacts with the German generals, his role as the one who recorded and presented their war histories to western readers, and his strong public support for them bound the generals to him by feelings of gratitude, self-interest, and dependency.[2]

Mearsheimer has fully exposed Liddell Hart's persistent efforts and elaborate techniques in using his connections with the German generals for extracting, inviting, and planting accolades, which he later blew out beyond their original context, modified, inserted in key publications, and disseminated widely by any possible means. The German generals' recognition of his influence was the chief means by which Liddell Hart sought (successfully) to resurrect his reputation after the sharp eclipse it had suffered after the fall of France and during the Second World War. As Mearsheimer has shown, three cases were of particular significance for Liddell Hart: Guderian, Rommel, and Manstein.

In Manstein's case Liddell Hart's efforts did not bear fruit, despite the fact that the field-marshal was heavily in his debt. Liddell Hart intervened to relieve the hardship and humiliation which Manstein endured in the prisoner-of-war camp. On Manstein's request he arranged for his wife and child to be transferred to his sister's house in the French zone of occupation in Germany. He campaigned against Manstein's being tried as a war criminal, assisted in his defence when he was put on trial, and fought for his release after he had been convicted. He took under his care the publication of the English edition of Manstein's war memoirs, *Lost Victories* (1958), and as late as the 1960s intervened to secure a place at Cambridge for Manstein's son. Yet, despite Manstein's gratitude, he withstood Liddell Hart's indirect attempts, through Manstein's lawyer and biographer, to make Liddell Hart the inspiration behind the Ardennes operation which Manstein had conceived and which had led to the Allies' collapse in the West in 1940. Liddell Hart, who in his interwar books had several times made the observation that the Ardennes were not impassable, wanted Manstein to endorse the sentence: 'he had been impressed, he said, by an article of Captain Liddell Hart's arguing that an armoured thrust through the Ardennes was technically possible'. But Manstein would specifically not concede to anything more than the non-committal: 'Captain Liddell Hart, he said, had suggested in an article before the war that an armoured thrust through the Ardennes was technically possible.' This did not stop Liddell Hart from putting his own words in Manstein's mouth in his *Memoirs*.[3]

Liddell Hart had more luck with Rommel's family. The field-marshal's widow and son were very anxious that Liddell Hart would edit an English edition of his papers. Rommel had many critics in the German army and general staff, who disputed his qualifications as a strategist and his conduct in North Africa and Normandy and who held that his abilities had been greatly exaggerated by the German and Allies' war propaganda. Liddell Hart clearly indicated in his first letter to Mrs Rommel that he would make a favourable case on his behalf. On his persistent urging Rommel's family and his chief of staff in North Africa, General Fritz Bayerlein, provided flimsy but reasonable evidence that Rommel, like most German officers, had known of Liddell Hart during the 1930s and had probably read some of his writings, though he himself had not been converted to armour before 1940. The evidence further showed that during the war Rommel had on two different occasions mentioned the failure of his British opponents to adopt the theories of armoured warfare originally developed by 'British military critics' (Bayerlein: Fuller and Liddell Hart). In one of his papers Rommel had also specifically referred to an article Liddell Hart had written during the war. Liddell Hart, however, did not accept the job of editing Rommel's papers before he extracted from Rommel's family and from Bayerlein statements that made Rommel nothing less than his 'pupil' who had been 'highly influenced by his tactical and strategic conceptions'. He inserted this statement in the English edition of *The Rommel Papers* (1953), but failed to make Bayerlein have it incorporated in the German one.[4]

The most important case for Liddell Hart and the one in which he won his crowning success was that of Guderian, Germany's foremost armour pioneer. The two corresponded extensively from September 1948, Liddell Hart questioning Guderian on the development of the Panzer arm and the conduct of the war. The brisk and abrasive Guderian had also made himself quite a number of enemies in the German army both before and during the war, and was interested in getting his side of the story told. *The Other Side of the Hill* had been published before he and Liddell Hart made contact, but Liddell Hart was planning a second, enlarged edition of the book. Six months after they began their correspondence he informed Guderian that he intended to devote a whole chapter to him in the new edition. At about the same time he inquired if Guderian had considered writing his war memoirs. Guderian, who was receiving no pension, was then living with his wife in one room under conditions of virtual poverty. As he wrote to Liddell Hart (who was also involved in the efforts to have the German generals' pensions restored), publishing his memoirs was for him, if nothing else, a means to earn a living.[5] Liddell Hart took it upon himself to find British and American publishers for the memoirs and also put Guderian in touch with British and American journals. Getting the memoirs accepted for publication in the West proved, however, very difficult. Two publishing houses, Collins and Cassell, successively rejected the typescript, describing it (rightly) as 'full of self-pity and unrepentant nationalism, typical of a German officer of the nationalistic school'.[6] Liddell Hart worked hard to soften and remove the problematic passages in the book, find another publisher and, finally, secure the best financial terms for Guderian. When the book, *Panzer Leader* (1952), became a best-seller, he asked for the 25% of the royalties which Guderian himself had offered him for his immense trouble. His request remained unanswered, for Guderian had just died.

As Mearsheimer has pointed out, the more Guderian's debt to Liddell Hart had grown, the more persistent Liddell Hart's inquiries became regarding his influence upon him, and the more did Guderian realize that he would have to contribute the kind of acknowledgement that Liddell Hart wanted to the mutually beneficial relationship. At the time Liddell Hart was taking the publication of Guderian's memoirs under his care and was promising Guderian that the chapter devoted to him in the new edition of *The Other Side of the Hill* would present him as more important than Hitler, he also sent him his critique of Fuller's *Lectures on FSR III* and indicated clearly, time and again, where he thought his own unique contribution to the theory of armoured warfare lay.[7] When Guderian failed to take up his hints, he resorted to more direct measures. In the German edition of Guderian's memoirs *Erinnerungen eines Soldaten* (1951) Guderian wrote the following paragraph:

> It was principally the books and articles of the Englishmen, Fuller, Liddell Hart and Martel, that excited my interest and gave me food for thought. These far-sighted soldiers were even then trying to make the tank more than just an infantry support weapon. They envisaged it in relation to the growing mechanization of our age, and thus they became the pioneers of a new type of warfare on the largest scale.

Going over the English translation of the book, Liddell Hart was unsatisfied. He wrote to Guderian:

I appreciate very much what you said in the paragraph.... So I am sure will Fuller and Martel. It is a most generous acknowledgement. But because of our special association, and the wish that I should write the foreword to your book, people may wonder why there is no separate reference to what my writings taught. You might care to insert a remark that I emphasized the use of armoured forces for long-range operations against the opposing army's communications, and also proposed a type of armoured division combining panzer and panzer-infantry units – and that these points particularly impressed you.

Coming after Liddell Hart's tremendous efforts over the publication and contract of the book, his request was not refused. Guderian inserted in *Panzer Leader* the following paragraph after the one he had originally written for the German edition:

> Further, it was Liddell Hart who emphasized the use of armoured forces for long-range strokes, operations against the opposing army's communications, and also proposed the type of armoured division combining panzer and panzer infantry units. Deeply impressed by these ideas I tried to develop them for our own army. So I owe many suggestions of our further development to Captain Liddell Hart.[8]

These famous lines established Liddell Hart's reputation for a generation as the inspiration behind the German 'Blitzkrieg'. Such strong evidence left little room for doubt, especially as Liddell Hart took care to cover his tracks. He apparently removed his letter to Guderian and Guderian's letter of agreement from his archive, and at least on one documented occasion, in reply to queries by an observant student, denied any knowledge of the reasons for the difference between the German and English editions of Guderian's memoirs. Only in the mid-1970s were the incriminating letters discovered in Guderian's records by his biographer, Kenneth Macksey, and placed back in Liddell Hart's archive.[9]

When manufactured evidence is revealed the damage to one's case might be fatal. Liddell Hart's claim for influence on the Germans has lost its credibility in the eyes of historians. At the very least it has become clear that he exaggerated this influence at the expense of Fuller and other British armour pioneers. At the same time, not only his case but British influence as a whole on the evolution of the

German Panzer arm, which previously was taken for granted, has now been called into question. And yet Liddell Hart's self-inflicted injury in trying to write the historical record himself does not close the case but merely opens it afresh. The fact that he was fraudulent does not necessarily mean that he was wholly incorrect. To establish how things really were, the evidence on the subject from the German sources of the interwar period itself must be looked into. This has simply never been done. Liddell Hart himself did not read German, and he was anyhow satisfied with what he had managed to extract from the German generals directly. His biographers, too, confined themselves solely to his own records. Only in recent years have historians, working on the other side of the hill on other subjects using the German documents, dug up some evidence relevant to our case. Although a great deal of the German archival material was destroyed by the war or lost, leaving considerable gaps in the record, the surviving material is substantial. In addition, open publications from the interwar period, particularly the general staff's semi-official *Militär-Wochenblatt*, a professional journal of high quality, provide a very useful and often parallel source which complements the official record.

There are many parallels between the current trends in the historiography of interwar British and German armour. As with Fuller and Liddell Hart in the former case, it has become apparent that Guderian monopolized the history of the Panzer arm. The many existing popular histories of the development of German armour merely paraphrase Guderian's *Panzer Leader*, and his biographers have not diverged from his own version either.[10] Surprisingly for a subject that has attracted so much interest, a full-scale scholarly history of the German Panzer arm, based on the documents, has yet to be written. Only in the mid-1960 were the documents returned to Germany from the United States, and even then, with the exception of a number of important contributions, German academics were discouraged by the universities from dealing with 'technical' military questions. This study can fill the gap only partly. It will attempt to outline the genesis of the Panzer arm and the growth of its operational doctrine, with special attention to the British influence on these developments, including that of Liddell Hart. As will be shown, this influence was indeed, after all, decisive.

I Origins: the 1920s and early 1930s

The first substantial modification to have been made in Guderian's version of the evolution of the Panzer arm concerns the notion that the German army's serious interest in armour was born, and had always been associated, with him. This is very far from the truth. Contrary to its popular image as professionally conservative, an image fostered by Guderian's memoirs, the Reichswehr showed lively interest in armour in the 1920s. At that time Guderian was only beginning to develop as an armour man and was still remote from positions of influence. A study of the Reichswehr in the Seeckt era has recently highlighted all this in considerable detail.[11] Compared with the Entente powers, Germany created a very small tank force only late in the First World War and came out of the war with little practical experience in tank warfare. The stipulations of the Versailles Treaty, which prevented Germany from building and possessing tanks, further fundamentally hindered her development in the field of armour. For both reasons, however, the Reichswehr's sensitivity to the new weapon was in some respects heightened. For both reasons it was also especially conscious of, and dependent upon, developments abroad, to a degree that no other great power's army was.

The German postwar field service regulations, *Leadership and Battle with Combined Arms* (1923), dedicated several sections to the tank. Taking their cue from the post-war doctrines of the French and British armies, the regulations envisaged the employment of the tank in two main roles. A heavy type would be used in large concentrations and even in formations of its own, on suitable ground and with the aid of surprise, as a decisive offensive weapon. It would lead the infantry in the breaking in battle of the enemy's fortified positions, closely cooperating with artillery, engineers, and aircraft. A light type, of which ideally a battalion would be assigned to each infantry division, would be used for reconnaissance and other cavalry-type missions; but for the exploitation of success into a war of movement, it, too, might be concentrated in large formations. The regulations also envisaged an anti-tank role and the role of counter-offensive in defence for the tank.[12] This was the standard picture in the postwar years in the leading tank countries regarding the future employment of armour.

The sections on the tank in the regulations were probably drafted by, or written in consultation with, Lieutenant Ernst Volckheim, a veteran of the First World War German tank force, who served after the war in the Inspectorate of Transport Troops (In.6). They are practically identical with his own publications. Writing extensively on tanks in articles and booklets, Volckheim was well recognized towards the middle of the 1920s as the Reichswehr's leading expert on the use of armour. He was well informed about the history of the tank in the First World War and the French and British postwar armour organization and doctrine, upon which he relied and which he introduced to German readers.[13] Germany's foremost expert on tank technology and another major source of information on the world's armour for German readers was the Austrian captain, engineer Fritz Heigl. Possessing an international reputation in the field, in the second half of the 1920s he regularly contributed technical surveys of the world's tanks to *Militär-Wochenblatt* (as well as to the *Journal of the Royal Tank Corps*). His *Pocket Book of Tanks* (1926) was the standard work on the subject which, expanded and updated by others after its author's premature death, ran into three editions before the war.[14]

Heigl also advised the German army on tanks.[15] In 1925–26 the Reichswehr issued preliminary specifications for the building of two experimental tank types, to be produced by German firms in secrecy in order to avoid detection by the Allies. These were code-named 'Heavy Tractor' and 'Light Tractor' – fast-heavy and medium-light types respectively. From 1929–30 the various models produced were secretly tested in the joint German–Soviet tank school in Kama, near Kazan.[16] Both types possessed high speed (30–35 km/h) and resembled the British Independent and Vickers Medium Tank respectively. Indeed, at the time they were initiated, attention in Germany was increasingly focusing on new and exciting developments in armoured warfare coming from Britain. By 1924–25, in his last publications before disappearing from the scene, Volckheim, who had previously been more influenced by the larger and closer French tank force, was beginning to whistle new tunes. He cited a British officer's criticism of the French army's lack of special inspectorate for tanks, and a British claim, following the latest French manoeuvres, that the French had made no progress in tank warfare since the war. He called attention to the heavily armed and fast (British) medium tank as a new significant development in the field and described its use in the 1924 British manoeuvres in cooperation with armoured cars and cavalry. In 1926 Heigl's survey of the world's tanks mentioned the new theories, specifically associated with Fuller, of using fast tanks with a large radius of action to revive the war of movement.[17]

The earliest significant introduction of the new British school to German readers was Liddell Hart's articles 'The Next Great War' and

'The Development of a "New Model" Army: Suggestions on a Progressive, but Gradual Mechanization', published in 1924. The former was abstracted as the opening piece of a July issue of *Militär-Wochenblatt*, whereas the latter received only a few lines in the regular military journals section in November but was described as 'very interesting for all concerned with the mechanization of modern armies' and recommended for a full translation into German.[18] Here, as always, the summaries in the German journal were accurate and to the point. A month later, without mentioning either Liddell Hart's name or Fuller's (from whom the former derived his ideas), another opening piece in *Militär-Wochenblatt* described the new thoughts in Britain of replacing the muscle armies by machine armies through gradual mechanization in several phases, ending with an all-armoured army and a reduction of 60 per cent in manpower. The article concluded that this programme would be tested in the next British summer manoeuvres in 1925. As was often the case in *Militär-Wochenblatt*, the summary was contributed by a general staff officer whose field of speciality covered the subject reviewed, and who for reasons of confidentiality signed only with a number.[19]

So Liddell Hart was basically correct in claiming that his earliest articles on armour had left an impression in Germany.[20] Yet this impression should be understood within a wider context. The older historiography, taking its cue from the writings of Fuller, Liddell Hart, and Guderian, emphasized the role of individuals and theories in the evolution of armour. For all their significance, however, armies are even more impressed and prompted into action by tangible developments in reality. It was only in combination with the path-breaking developments in tank design and armour organization in Britain, which were actually being tested in large-scale manoeuvres, that the British pioneering theories of armoured warfare, which had been a necessary condition for these developments in the first place, attracted so much attention in Germany and in other great powers' armies.

In late 1924 the intelligence branch of the German covert general staff (*Truppenamt*) surveyed the previous summer's British manoeuvres, the first large-scale manoeuvres to be held in Britain after the war. In the section dealing with tanks and motorized troops the survey highlighted the appearance of the new Vickers Medium Tank, armed with a 3-pounder and capable of a revolutionary 35 km/h. The survey emphasized the tank's potential for use in a war of movement and noted a tension in this respect between the older and younger officers in the British army, the latter regarding the new tank as 'all mighty'. The motorization on lorries of some of the other forces was also noted.[21] *Militär-Wochenblatt* published a summary of the survey, making the same points. It was written by the same general staff officer who three weeks earlier had described in the journal the new thoughts in Britain regarding the employment of armour.[22]

In the following years close attention to British theory and practice was strongly evident in the German army. Reports on and references to the revolutionary characteristics of the Vickers Medium Tank were unceasing, intertwined with reports on British manoeuvres. A short review in *Militär-Wochenblatt* of the 1925 manoeuvres described the use of the tank in semi-independent roles. It was written that the British were investing a great deal of attention in the idea of tanks breaking through to the enemy's artillery zone, followed and supported by armoured infantry. This was the modern tank battle, was the conclusion.[23] In 'A Reflection on the Employment of the Tank', a German officer wrote that the development of the tank since the war, embodied in the Medium Tank's speed and radius of action, opened new possibilities beyond its use for infantry support. This, stated the article, was the opinion of the British Colonel Fuller. Future war would be conducted by mechanized divisions in which all arms would be mechanized and armoured.[24] Several months later the same officer reported an article on the armour manoeuvres in *The Daily Telegraph* by 'Captain Liddell Hart, known from his book *Paris*'. The report highlighted the potential of the modern tank as against the views of the 'old school'.[25] Yet another article, 'The Impact of Modern Tanks on the Conduct of War', compared the British tanks and the British manoeuvres to the French. It stressed the great value of fast mechanized formations and described the British Medium Tank as the most advanced in the world, possessing amazing speed and radius of action. 'It has developed into the pure offensive weapon of the war of movement'. Wide-range drives have now become possible. The Germans, the article concluded, must take up the subject without delay.[26]

The acute awareness in Germany of the inextricable link between theories and practice in the development of British armour is apparent in the passages cited. A summary of Liddell Hart's *Paris* opened an issue of *Militär-Wochenblatt* in September 1926. His reports, particularly in *The Daily Telegraph*, were regularly cited.[27] An article by Tim Pile in *The Journal of the Royal Artillery* was summarized as 'British Views on the Development and Employment of Tanks', arguing that the tank would revolutionize war and stressing the differences from the French approach.[28] Fuller was slower to leave his mark in print in Germany, though experts were well aware both of his background with the Tank Corps in the First World War and of his paramount role in the new British school of armoured warfare. He was occasionally cited, but his earlier books were introduced to German readers somewhat belatedly. It was only his nomination in 1926 as assistant to the CIGS Milne with a special mandate for the advancement of mechanization that finally put him in the spotlight.[29] His *Reformation of War* (1923) was now picked up and summarized in *Militär-Wochenblatt* and, extensively, in three issues devoted almost entirely to it, in the general staff's foreign military literature journal.[30] His *Tanks in the Great War* was translated some time during the 1920s and circulated in typescript for internal use.[31]

To be sure, the Reichswehr was monitoring all armies and all foreign military publications on a grand scale. British armour developments and British manoeuvres were being reported, but so also were the French, Polish, Czechoslovakian, Soviet, Italian, American, Japanese, and those of at least a dozen smaller countries, inside and outside Europe. Articles and books by Fuller and Liddell Hart were summarized, but so were works by numerous other military writers from many countries.[32] And yet there was a difference. By 1925–27 enthusiasm in the Reichswehr for the British advances in armoured warfare was reaching fever pitch, both in official and more popular circles. Fuller and Liddell Hart in particular were becoming household names.

In a confidential memorandum in May 1926 Werner Blomberg, head of the operations branch in the German general staff, cited the British secretary of state for war's statement in Parliament that exercises had proven that the horse and the tank did not combine well; that the horse would be retained mainly for non-European theatres; that the British army would be gradually mechanized; and that a small mechanized force would be created immediately. The conclusion was: 'the British are the most advanced in mechanization'. A summary of the official document also appeared in *Militär-Wochenblatt*.[33] In October 1926 the British July manoeuvres, in which a regular infantry brigade was confronted by one composed of cavalry, mobile artillery, and a company of the Vickers Medium Tank, was reviewed in the journal. The review was based on Liddell Hart's reports in *The Daily Telegraph*. It also cited his own lessons from the manoeuvre, among them the maxim: 'move in dispersed order' (quoted in English); the importance of radio communication; and the conclusion that only mobile artillery can keep pace with the tanks.[34] In November 1926 a memorandum signed by General Heye, Seeckt's successor as commander in chief of the German army (*Chef der Heeresleitung*), again elaborated on the potential of the new tanks as revealed in the manoeuvres (speed: 30–45 km/h; range: 193 km). The memorandum asserted that the French possessed a large number of tanks which were, however, obsolescent, dating back to the war, whereas the British had got rid of their old models. The British used their tanks to attack the enemy's rear, reserves, command posts, and artillery.[35] A change in German doctrine soon followed. 'By late 1926 a directive set forth that tank units could be separated from a "slowly moving infantry" and that tanks could be best used either in conjunction with "mobile troops or as independent units".' In January 1927 a memorandum signed by the Head of the Operations Branch (T1) in the General Staff, Werner von Fritsch, stated: 'Armoured, quickly moving tanks most probably will become the operationally decisive offensive weapon. From an operational perspective this weapon will be most effective if concentrated in independent units like tank brigades.' The document recommended the gradual conversion of German motorized transportation into fighting units.[36]

The climax of the new British advances in the field of armoured warfare and of the German interest in them was, of course, the first trials of the Experimental Mechanized Force in the summer of 1927. In April a report in *Militär-Wochenblatt* cited Liddell Hart's prescriptions for the brigade in *The Daily Telegraph*. The brigade, he wrote, ought to operate independently against far-away targets. It should be used as the mobile reserve and decisive arm of manoeuvre in the hands of the commander in chief.[37] The manoeuvre itself was described in the journal in four consecutive issues, in full detail, day by day, complete with maps.[38] A later report by the Inspectorate of Transport Troops defined the tank force's main role in the manoeuvres as follows: it was to operate in combination with cavalry and with other mechanized forces as the army's reserve, or for long-range reconnaissance, or for surprise attack on the enemy's flank and rear.[39] Milne's Tidworth address at the end of the manoeuvres was summarized in the general staff's foreign literature journal from Liddell Hart's report in *The Daily Telegraph* and also cited in *Militär-Wochenblatt* from Liddell Hart's report in the *Journal of the Royal Tanks Corps*. Armoured divisions would be created in the future, promised the British CIGS. 'With the opening of a campaign the armoured force will penetrate 300–450 km [200–300 miles] deep into enemy territory' or circle around its strategic flank. The writer in *Militär-Wochenblatt* called attention to the address as expressing the views of the British general staff.[40] The German journal also announced the publication in Britain and summarized the content of *Provisional Instructions for Tank and Armoured Car Training* (1927). As Guderian would write in reference to 1928: 'the current English handbook on armoured fighting vehicles was translated into German and for many years served as the theoretical manual for our developing ideas'. The manual was sold freely in Britain by His Majesty's Stationery Office. In due course, the Germans would also get hold of the confidential pioneering *Mechanized and Armoured Formations* (1929) and its successor, *Modern Formations* (1931).[41] Finally, reporting on the plans for the second season of the Armoured Force's trials in 1928, *Militär-Wochenblatt* cited a British source who predicted that the mechanization reforms would be carried through after the trials, which would signify 'victory for the mechanization school, for which writers like Colonel Fuller, Captain Liddell Hart and Colonel Rowan-Robinson have done so much.'[42]

In 1927 Liddell Hart's article in *The Daily Telegraph*, 'The Remaking of Modern Armies', was summarized in the general staff's foreign military literature journal. The book bearing the same title was extensively summarized a year later in two issues dedicated almost entirely to it, and also, in considerable detail, in *Militär-Wochenblatt*.[43] Fuller's *On Future Warfare* (1928) was summarized, a chapter each, in eight issues of the foreign-literature journal, after an introductory review by Liddell Hart in *The Daily Telegraph* following its publication.[44] Articles by and references to the two British military writers regularly appeared in German journals.[45] Their books published in Britain were prominently reviewed in *Militär-Wochenblatt* (which was uncommon for books in foreign languages), often in special review articles rather than in the regular book review section, and normally in very complimentary terms.[46] Some criticisms, mainly of Fuller's ideas, recognized as the source and senior figure of the new school, were also printed, though the general picture remained one of absorbing interest.[47] Articles by other British armour pioneers such as Swinton, Martel, Hobart, Broad, and Rowan-Robinson, were also occasionally cited during the second half of the 1920s,[48] and there were, for example, lengthy summaries of books by William Robertson and Herbert Richmond. As mentioned before, other countries were also extensively covered. All the same, Fuller and Liddell Hart were in a league of their own, both in the quantity of coverage and acclaim. An index of the general staff's foreign military literature journal shows Fuller and Liddell Hart occupying the lion's share of the section 'Future Warfare' in the late 1920s.[49] At first, introductory references in German journals spoke of 'Captain Liddell Hart, known from his book *Paris*', or 'Captain Liddell Hart, who has made a name for himself in Britain as a military writer'; but soon it was to be always the formula 'the well-known Captain Liddell Hart', or simply 'Liddell Hart' – an old acquaintance who needed no introduction. A survey in *Militär-Wochenblatt* of an issue of the RUSI Journal described his article '1927 or 527' with the words: 'a brief presentation of the author's well-known views'.[50] Nothing more was needed. Things were similar with Fuller. General Blumentritt's recollection of the period, though written after the Second World War, seems to capture the feeling of the time:

> Liddell Hart and Fuller were for us young officers after 1920 'the modern military authors'. Particularly in the Reichswehr they were carefully studied and all their articles read. In those days we were lieutenants and captains aged 28 to 35 and took delight in the modern spirit of these writers.[51]

To an even greater degree than in Britain, the rise of Fuller and – more dramatically, considering his starting position – Liddell Hart, from anonymity to fame in professional circles in Germany was meteoric, taking barely more than a couple of years.

All this was part of a wider trend. In the second half of the 1920s the theme of future warfare was second in prominence only to the First World War on the pages of *Militär-Wochenblatt*. Within future warfare, mechanized and armoured warfare was matched only by air warfare, another subject attracting lively interest. The Reichswehr was entering new fields. Following the German manoeuvres of 1928 which tested the army's armament needs for the period 1928–33, the decision to convert the motorized transportation units into combat units was finally taken.[52] In 1929, as the Chief of Staff of the Inspectorate of Motorized Troops, Colonel Oswald Lutz, was summarizing the data on mechanization in Britain,[53] Blomberg, now the chief of the general staff (*Truppenamt*), was drafting plans for the creation of mechanized formations. The document spoke of 'independent tank formations, the line of development practically tried out in several foreign armies'. It laid out the structures for an independent tank regiment and an independent motorized infantry unit, and asked for the necessary vehicles.[54]

To add weight to his proposals, Blomberg's memorandum mentioned developments in 'several foreign armies'. Indeed by 1929, prompted by the British example, which had been attentively watched by the general staffs of all the great powers, seminal trials in mechanization had been initiated by other armies as well. In 1928, on the instruction of the Secretary of State for War, D. Davis, who had witnessed the British 1927 manoeuvres, the United States' army formed and tried out for the first time its own experimental armoured brigade. The French were quickening the mechanization of their cavalry.[55] The Italians, too, were closely studying and much influenced by the British manoeuvres.[56] The first Soviet mechanized regiments were created in 1929, and the concept of 'deep battle' was evolved from 1928–29 onward, stimulated initially by the British pioneering advances, though taking its own interesting and largely independent course. Blomberg, who visited the Red Army in 1928, was deeply impressed by the vigour of the Soviet state, though, significantly for our case, criticized the Soviet tanks for lack of speed.[57] As we have already seen, it was to the leading British model that German eyes were turned.

In view of Blomberg's prominent involvement in the developments described, it comes as no surprise that at the Disarmament Conference in Geneva where he headed the German military delegation, he asked to meet Liddell Hart and told him of his admiration for his work. For obvious reasons Blomberg did not mention the British influence on the clandestine evolution of German armour. Instead, he discussed with Liddell Hart the latter's ideas in *Foch* regarding flexible defence, a problem with which the small and manoeuvre-oriented Reichswehr was preoccupied, especially on the eastern border, where Blomberg was now the commander in East Prussia.[58] Later that year Walter Reichenau, Blomberg's chief of staff in East Prussia, wrote to Liddell Hart, informing him that he was translating *Foch*: 'Here I found a new and unusually high standard of judgement, not following obsolete theories, but setting new rules – if there are any at all.'[59] Colonel Sir Andrew Thorne, the British military attaché in Berlin from 1932 to 1935, recalled after the war:

> during that time there I could not fail to be impressed by the extent to which both Liddell Hart's and 'Boney' Fuller's books were being studied by officers of all ranks and arms in the German Army. I knew both Blomberg (Minister of War) and Reichenau (Chief of the Defence Staff) very well, and they were both engaged in translating

books by these two authors for use for non-English speaking German officers. They frequently sought my help to elucidate some point which was not quite clear to them.[60]

As Guderian was to testify, the promotion of Blomberg and Reichenau following Hitler's rise to power had 'an immediate effect on my work. Both these generals favoured modern ideas, and so I now found considerable sympathy for the ideas of the armoured force, at least at the highest levels of the Wehrmacht'. In 1938 Reichenau assumed command over Group Command 4, the army incorporating all the then existing armoured and mechanized corps of the German army.[61]

It is time for a few words of summary on the influence of Fuller and Liddell Hart on the growth of the incipient German doctrine of armoured warfare during the second half of the 1920s. Although mostly prompted into action by tangible developments in British tank design, armour organization, and annual manoeuvres, the Reichswehr's primary access to these developments was through written, predominantly open sources. In the 1920s it was not even allowed to have a military attaché in Britain, but in contrast to Germany there was no difficulty in crystallizing a fairly complete picture of the British army from monitoring newspaper reports and Parliamentary deliberations. It was therefore only to be expected that those in Britain who found greater expression in print were far more recognized in Germany than other, 'practical men', out of the limelight. This meant that Fuller and Liddell Hart enjoyed by far the highest profile, though other armour pioneers were also known as far as they published. Fuller was from the outset recognized as both the leading British armour practitioner and theorist, and from 1926 onward everything he wrote – even the most metaphysical and fanciful articles – was immediately seized upon in Germany. Liddell Hart, who in the mid-1920s had better access to print and who wrote prolifically and very lucidly, was slightly ahead in making his impact in Germany as a theorist, and his perceptive observations and ideas in the field of armoured warfare would always be regarded with great esteem in the Reichswehr. In addition, his columns in *The Daily Telegraph* remained a major source of information on all things military in Britain throughout the period. As mentioned before, until the mid-1930s Liddell Hart was the only permanent military correspondent in a British newspaper, the other newspapers employing special military correspondents mainly for the summer manoeuvres. In conclusion, Fuller and Liddell Hart were highly influential in

Germany through three main channels: directly as theorists of modern mechanized war; indirectly through the influence of their theories and actions on the development of British armour which from the mid-1920s was increasingly becoming a model for emulation for the Reichswehr; and as sources of information on British armour developments in the First World War and the interwar period.

Finally, how does Guderian fit into all this? As one historian has recently put it: 'Guderian is, at this point, just another general staff officer who supported ... [the] new doctrine of mobile (tank) warfare as a means to overcome the impasse of the *Vernichtungsgedanke* in World War I.'[62] And even this assessment only really applies from the late 1920s. Even Guderian's own memoirs, if stripped of their strongly subjective perspective by being placed into a more general frame, testify to that, for on the whole they are accurate, and distort mainly by selection and omission. Guderian was posted to the Inspectorate of Transport Troops as a captain in 1922 without any prior familiarity with the subject. The motorized units were predominantly concerned at the time with transportation, mainly of supplies, as was Guderian in his assignments with the troops and at headquarters. He took part in a number of trials and exercises in 1922–24, only slowly developing an interest in the combat-potential of motorization. In the first place, motorized transportation required protection against aircraft and also, when travelling through the battle zone, against ground troops. This, Guderian thought, could be provided by guns, armoured cars, and other mechanized combat troops. It was on these humble problems that he wrote his first short articles, published in *Militär-Wochenblatt* in 1924–25. Tanks, forbidden to Germany, were still practically beyond his scope.[63] Only in 1924 was Guderian entrusted with the responsibility for a series of exercises, 'intended to explore the possibilities of the employment of tanks, particularly for reconnaissance duties in connection with cavalry'.[64] Searching out solutions for the problems with which he was grappling, he began to explore the literature on mechanized warfare more widely, literature which was inevitably mostly foreign. He was introduced to it by Volckheim. 'The English and French had had far greater experience in the field and had written much more about it. I got hold of their books, and I learnt.'[65] The original paragraph Guderian would write in his memoirs concerning the influence of the writings of Fuller, Liddell Hart, and Martel, in that order, is unquestionably authentic.[66] For example, Guderian informed Liddell Hart that as far as he could recall he had first read his articles around 1923–24.[67] After what we have seen above, there is no reason to doubt this evidence (the latter year being the correct one), especially as Guderian had not been hinted before by Liddell Hart regarding the publication dates of his earliest works on armoured warfare. Furthermore, at the time Liddell Hart's articles were prominently summarized in *Militär-Wochenblatt*, Guderian wrote his first articles for that journal and established close relations with its editor.[68]

From late 1924 to late 1928, the years German attention was turning to British armour theory and practice and the first steps were being taken to emulate them, Guderian was away from the Inspectorate of Transport Troops and from involvement in decision-making. He was posted to the Army's Training Branch and sent to the staff of an infantry division as instructor for tactics and military history.[69] By late 1928, he wrote, as 'I returned to my preoccupation with tanks ... I was still lacking in all practical experience of tanks; at that time I had never seen the inside of one.' He derived practically everything he knew about them from a study of foreign literature.[70] By late 1927, reflecting the direction German military thought had been taking, Guderian, too, arrived at the conclusion that the tank, aided by other mechanized arms and by aircraft, was the means for a renewal of the war of movement. Permanent mechanized formations were needed.[71] For some unknown reason and against the printed evidence, Guderian's memoirs date this decisive step in his development to 1929:

> I became convinced that tanks working on their own or in conjunction with infantry could never achieve decisive importance. My historical studies, the exercises carried out in England and our own experiences with mock-ups had persuaded me that tanks would never be able to produce their full effect until the other weapons on whose support they must inevitably rely were brought up to their standard of speed and cross-country performance ... what was needed were armoured divisions which would include all the supporting arms needed to allow the tanks to fight with full effect.[72]

These were the ideas Blomberg, Heye, Fritsch, and others in the army's high command, most notably the first named, had already been officially endorsing and working for. Yet Guderian's memoirs only hint cursorily at some of this,[73] either because he was egocentric; or because he was not fully aware of these developments, being at that crucial period away from the centre of activity; or because of his reluctance even in the early 1950s to discuss unlawful German planning –

he did not mention the cooperation with the Soviet Union and the Kazan armour school either (possibly because of the Cold War climate), though he did refer to the clandestine German experimental tank production; or, finally, because he did not think the 'prehistory' of the Panzer arm, before it was actually created in the 1930s, deserved more space.[74] In conclusion, Guderian merely took part in a much wider movement within German military thought from the mid-1920s toward the idea, adopted from the British, of operationally decisive armoured formations. Furthermore, his contribution to the development of that idea in Germany was at first very limited.

Things entered a new stage with the beginning of a new decade. After the 1928 manoeuvres the British disbanded the experimental armoured brigade and would create new armoured formations and carry out new trials only at intervals. At the same time, the Germans were moving towards rearmament, a process finally set in motion with Hitler's rise to power.[75] Earlier schemes were now beginning to materialize, including the creation of a German armoured force, which still looked up to the British as its model. Lastly, Guderian was rising in rank and increasingly moving into positions of influence. His case really begins with his nomination in the autumn of 1931 to the position of chief of staff to the new Inspector of Motorized Troops, General Oswald Lutz. In this position Guderian became the main driving force of the inspectorate in the very years that rearmament and the expansion of the German army made the creation of Panzer divisions (and later corps) a real possibility. It hardly needs emphasizing that there was a wealth of difference between widespread awareness and even enthusiastic acceptance of the potential of such formations in theory, as shared by leading circles in the Reichswehr's high command in the second half of the 1920s, and the actual creation of the force with all the intricate problems and crucial decisions involved.

Something of the developments behind the scenes was reflected by *Militär-Wochenblatt*. In the early 1930s the journal was publishing imaginary tactical problems on 'The Employment of an Independent Panzer Formation' (brigade size), and printing various schemes put forward in foreign professional periodicals for the structure of the armoured formation. As before, it was mainly to Britain that German eyes were turned.[76] An article comparing the British and French tank manuals emphasized the differences between their respective approaches. The British one (1927), it was written, prescribed the mobile and concentrated employment of tanks, in combination with other mobile forces or wholly independently.[77] A comprehensive survey, 'The Tanks of the Present', opened with the statement that 'with its elite Tank Corps Britain is the most modern country in tank tactics'. While France was also strong in equipment, Britain led the world in the production of medium tanks.[78] Another survey of 'The New Fast Mobile Formation' in European armies called it a British invention which was now being taken up by all countries.[79] An article, 'An Independent Armoured Brigade in Battle', citing the British manual 'Mechanized and Armoured Formations' (1929), stated: 'Britain has been the country which has most notably developed the new arm. It is therefore understandable that the rest of the world's armies pay much attention to the trials held in Britain.'[80]

The 1931 manoeuvres of the British armoured brigade under Broad's command were covered by *Militär-Wochenblatt*, which described them as 'the strongest concentration of tank formations since the war'.[81] Following the 1932 manoeuvres British sources were cited to the effect that the range of which tanks were now capable was up to 240 km.[82] A survey of the manoeuvres, based on 'British journals', described the outflanking move of the armoured brigade against an infantry division. The latter was reported destroyed. One of the conclusions cited was the option of the brigade being employed deep into the enemy's rear, either independently or in cooperation with infantry and cavalry, to cut off his communications.[83] A large opening article with pictures, 'The Mechanization of the British Army', started with the words: 'The British army undoubtedly stands today ahead of all armies in the field of mechanization.... The frequent manoeuvres of the armoured formations at Salisbury are today the object of curiosity for all men of cultivation. They are in fact the highest school of mechanization.' The article reported that the British tank brigade was intended for independent raids behind the enemy's position, with the motorized infantry and cavalry moving in its wake to secure and hold the ground occupied by the tanks. The tank brigade was reckoned to advance in leaps of up to 150 km a day. Its operations would resemble those of sea warfare.[84] From 1932 Major Walter Nehring was first staff officer responsible for organization in the Inspectorate of Motorized Troops (*erster Generalstabsoffizier (Ia) für Fragen der Organisation*) under Lutz and Guderian. His first little book on armoured warfare (1934), referring to the British as the leaders in the field, described the 1932 manoeuvres. It stressed the Tank Brigade's employment for independent strategic (*operativ*) missions under a system of radio control.[85]

The surviving documents of the German general staff depict a similar picture from behind the scenes. A fully detailed, day by day survey of the armour manoeuvres of 1932, complete with maps and organization tables, was composed by the intelligence branch, signed by the Chief of the General Staff (*Truppenamt*) General Adam, and distributed in 250 copies.[86] The authors of the survey, who stressed the importance of the manoeuvres, complained that the reports available to them (not cited) still only made possible the most general picture. From 1933, however, this problem was remedied, for Germany now possessed a military attache in London. The first to hold the post was Colonel, later Major-General Baron Geyer von Schweppenburg. His political and military reports from Britain received the closest attention from, and were highly valued by, the Chief of the General Staff from late 1933, General Ludwig Beck.[87] One of Geyer's first despatches to Berlin was a British official briefing of the tank brigade's manoeuvres of 1932.[88] Commenting on another of Geyer's early dispatches, an overall report on the British army, German intelligence concluded in respect to armour: 'General judgement: the British know that in their tanks they have a valuable weapon. There is an apparent tendency to rely on the effect of tanks against flanks and rear.'[89] In March 1934, in a new report on the state of the British army, Geyer wrote: 'In the mixed tank brigade the British army created the most important mobile "modern formation", which it holds to be necessary for powerful, long range, all out strikes.' He further assessed that in creating a tank battalion in Egypt the foundation was laid for the creation of a second 'modern formation' – the light tank brigade.[90]

In October 1934 Geyer reported in full detail on the pioneering armour manoeuvres of that year, in which the Tank Brigade and experimental Mobile Division under Hobart and Lindsay respectively for the first time tried out sweeping strategic penetrations.[91] A few days before, *Militär-Wochenblatt* had already printed a concise but highly informative survey of the manoeuvres. The tank brigade, it was written, 'used its high mobility to strike deep into the enemy's territory ... a city was fixed as an important strategic target deep behind the enemy's front, where arms factories, a big railway station, and the enemy's main headquarters were located'.[92] Of curiosity interest perhaps, at a later date the journal's exercise in translation from English read: 'The task given to the Mobile Force was to carry out a raid against various objectives – headquarters, ammunition depots, aerodromes etc. – lying in an area of about 140 square miles. The raid entailed a penetration of some 60 miles into enemy country.'[93] In

December the general staff issued its own conclusive report, signed by Chief of Staff Beck and again distributed in 250 copies.[94] We shall return to this later on.

Geyer was attending the British manoeuvres himself and was regularly meeting with leading British politicians and military men. He, too, however, derived a great deal of the information he passed on to Berlin from British newspaper reports, of which those by Liddell Hart in *The Daily Telegraph* held a prominent place. During the early 1930s articles and books by Fuller and Liddell Hart continued to be regularly printed in German professional journals, receiving the highest acclaim.[95] Again, *Militär-Wochenblatt* was using extracts from their writings in its regularly featured exercises in translation from English.[96] Of the two, Fuller was universally recognized as the father of the new British school.[97] By now, however, he was going into retirement and, although remarkably alert and prolific, was withdrawing from active involvement with the Tank Corps.[98] By contrast, Liddell Hart was tightening his association with the Tank Brigade as it was beginning its most ambitious manoeuvres yet. Both as a writer and through his personal connections in the army and War Office he was now constantly hammering his most cherished theme – the strategic, long-range use of armour. Geyer could not have known of his close cooperation with Hobart during the mid-1930s, but he realized his special position all the same.

In October 1933 Geyer sent to Berlin an article by Liddell Hart in *The Daily Telegraph* on the deficiencies of the British army in modern equipment. In the covering letter he wrote: 'Following my report on Liddell Hart's role in the life of the British army (report no. 7, p. 3), I enclose a very informative article of his, which appeared after I had written my comments on the British army.' Geyer further wrote that Liddell Hart's well-known train of thought notwithstanding, the article can be taken as a mouthpiece for the younger generation in the British army. Unfortunately, Geyer's original report, dated 30 September 1933, including his original references to Liddell Hart and commented upon extensively by German intelligence, has apparently been lost.[99] In April 1934 Geyer reported on the creation of a support battalion in every infantry brigade in Britain. He again noted that Liddell Hart (name underlined), the source of the information, 'has a favoured relationship with the War Office'.[100]

As he gained experience in Britain, Geyer's wisely discriminating attitude to Liddell Hart's writings sharpened. In November 1934, sending to Berlin reports from *The Morning Post* on the reorganization of the British army, he praised the newspaper's military correspondent as very serious and highly regarded in the War Office. In this respect, he wrote, he was like Liddell Hart, except that he wrote in a sober and dry manner, not as a self-styled prophet of a doctrine.[101] It was, however, precisely in that aspect of his writings that Liddell Hart had no substitute. Thus, in April 1935 Geyer reported the publication of Liddell Hart's *When Britain Goes to War*: 'From the book I call the immediate attention of In.6 [the Inspectorate of Motorized Troops; A.G.] to the description of the last years' manoeuvres of the tank units (pages 223, 274, 281) [1931, 1932, and 1934 respectively; A.G.]. A short discussion of the trials of the tanks in September 1934 [the experimental Mobile Division; A.G.] is to be found on page 293.' Several days later Geyer replied to queries sent to him by In.6 in Berlin regarding the 1934 British armour manoeuvres (queries not in the file). In reply to one query he wrote that the answer could perhaps be found in page 293 of Liddell Hart's *When Britain Goes to War*. A week later he confirmed that the book had been sent to Berlin.[102] The comments of the German reviewer of the book in *Militär-Wochenblatt* are also worth quoting:

> Extraordinarily interesting, particularly for the leaders of our new Panzer formations, are the chapters in which the tactical trials over the years of the British tank brigades on the classical Aldershot training ground are described. The development of the experimental mechanized and armoured formations from 1918 to 1935 is especially emphasized. Like Zeus's sun light and rain he bestows in describing the tactical missions in Aldershot love and blame on the leaders of the armoured formations.[103]

The reviewer concluded that 'the book should as quickly as possible be translated into German', which it was in the following year.

In the summer of 1935 the British manoeuvres again involved the Tank Brigade. The new professional journal published by the German war office mentioned that an infantry formation tried out cooperation with tanks, but also that 'the 1st Tank Brigade was exercised at the end of August as an independent armoured formation. As far as is known from newspaper reports, it was also employed in situations within which armoured formations, disengaged far from the main forces, attacked the enemy's artillery and rear communications.'[104] In October 1935 Geyer sent his detailed report on the manoeuvres. He noted a growing opposition to the tank formation.[105] In December the intelligence branch of the German general staff, composed its own even more comprehensive report, only partly relying on the attaché's report. Liddell Hart's articles in *The Times* featured here most prominently. As usual, he needed no introduction. Among the many references to his reports and judgements were the following:

> Liddell Hart highly praises the fact that in these exercises the tanks were assigned a strategic [*operativ*] mission. In his view it is against the nature of the armoured arm [*Panzer-Waffe*] to be solely employed as a tactical assistant of infantry. According to Liddell Hart's opinion, the employment of the armoured brigade was not very fortunate. It should have been used further north in order to press more strongly on the enemy's rear communications. Besides, the danger that the brigade would get involved in a costly *tactical* battle would thereby have been diminished.

And again:

> According to Liddell Hart, the enemy's artillery is not the right target for the armoured brigade. The attack on artillery is too risky and requires an especially skilled battle technique from the tanks ... More successful would be an attack on the rear communications. Liddell Hart holds in the rest of his interpretation that armoured formations should be entirely *freed from their unarmoured baggage train*, or else the advantage of their mobility over great distances might be lost.[106]

Although carefully collecting every piece of evidence testifying to his fame and influence, Liddell Hart was only generally aware at the time of this close attention to his writings, and would never have the specific details even later. In 1933 Sir Maurice Hankey, Secretary of the Committee of Imperial Defence, informed him: 'I heard from a high military authority in Berlin the other day that your and Fuller's writings are widely read and eagerly awaited throughout the German army.'[107] Liddell Hart and Fuller (who did not figure in Geyer's reports) dined with Geyer in 1934, but such correspondence as Liddell Hart and the German attaché had was formal. In July 1935 Geyer consulted Berlin on whether to invite Liddell Hart to attend the German manoeuvres (Fuller, a fascist and friendly to Nazi Germany, was invited and attended). He wrote that *The Times* had the leading military reports and that it was now in general very pro-German, but added: 'I do not hold Liddell Hart himself to be truly friendly to Germany.' Invitations were issued, but for some reason Liddell Hart declined. When Geyer left London in 1937 he informed Liddell Hart that he had been given command of a Panzer division, but only after the war did he resume contact with Liddell Hart in a very friendly manner. He was the translator of Liddell Hart's *Memoirs* into German.[108]

The period discussed above was of course the one in which the German general staff and In.6 headed by Lutz and Guderian (from the spring of 1934 onward simultaneously also head and chief of staff respectively of the newly created Command of the Motorized Troops; from late 1935: Command of the Panzer Troops) were working out and experimenting with the shape and role of the new Panzer units. The light, interim models, Panzer I and II, were beginning to come off the production line in 1934 and 1935 respectively, and the first three Panzer divisions were established in October 1935. Again the model for this development was clear. Colonel Sir Andrew Thorne, the British military attaché in Berlin between 1932 to 1935, in whose house Guderian had been a guest, told Liddell Hart in 1942 that the Germans had copied everything from Fuller and from him and that this had been common knowledge in Germany.[109] In 1958 Peter Paret recalled that it had been said in Berlin in the 1930s that Chief of the General Staff Beck wished six months could pass without him having to hear the name Liddell Hart.[110] But one does not have to rely solely on Liddell Hart's later records. As Thorne's words indicate, German sources of the time made no secret of whom they were trying to emulate. Guderian wrote in *Achtung Panzer!* (1937): 'After mature consideration it was decided that until we had accumulated sufficient experience on our own account, we should base ourselves principally on the British notions as expressed in *Provisional Instructions for Tank and Armoured Car Training* II 1927.'[111] In 1934 Major Walter Nehring, head of organization in the Inspectorate of Motorized Troops, wrote programmatically that the future belonged to the British independent and strategic (*operativ*) use of armour in cooperation with aircraft.[112] And after a visit to Berlin in 1935 Sir John Dill reported that he had been told by Lutz 'that the German tank corps had been modelled on the British'.[113]

II The creation of the Panzer arm

Before returning to the British influence on the Germans, we must turn to another contentious historical question: who exactly in Germany deserves the credit for the creation of the Panzer arm? Hitler, War Minister Blomberg, the Head of the Ministerial Office Reichenau, and the Army's Commander in Chief Fritsch either supported or were sympathetic to the creation of large armoured formations. But by the German system of command the man whose responsibility it was to plan out such things was the Chief of the Army's General Staff, General Ludwig Beck. According to Guderian, he was conservative, in the mould of the old Moltke school, had no understanding of modern technology, and objected to the idea of Panzer formations larger than brigades or to the strategic (*operativ*) employment of armour.[114] Historians, however, challenge this picture, in part or even in whole.

Beck has always been highly regarded as an intelligent and able chief of staff. Like most German officers he supported the National Socialist rise to power as a means to regenerate the German nation, revise Versailles, and restore Germany's status as a great power. By 1938, however, after the German high command had been informed by Hitler of his plans for expansion and war, Beck did his utmost during the Czechoslovakian crisis to reverse German policy, resigning his position when his efforts failed. He became the most distinguished figure behind the schemes to overthrow Hitler and was to find his death following the abortive coup of July 1944. In contrast to Guderian, who was typical of the younger generation of German officers, he was convinced that open German aggression would lead to a general war which Germany was bound to lose in the long run, because it would be crushed by the economic weight of the coalition that would form against her. For all that, politics *per se* had little to do with whatever differences Beck and Guderian had regarding the Panzer arm.[115] As historians now agree, in the mid-1930s Beck, too, was wholly committed to the creation of an 'offensive army' which would strengthen Germany's hand in the revision of the Versailles order.

Erich von Manstein, who as the head of the operations branch (*Abt. I*) from 1935 and deputy chief of the general staff (*Oberquartiermeister I*) in 1936–8 had been Beck's right hand man and had admired him deeply, very sensibly presented in his memoirs his chief's case (and his own) against Guderian's charges. Like other contemporaries, Manstein, who was in the best position to know, did not hesitate to describe Guderian as 'the man who is rightly regarded the creator of the German Panzer arm.... Nobody familiar with the development of this question would dispute that without Guderian's tenacity and combative temperament, the German army would not have had the Panzer arm, upon which its success in the first war years largely rested.' Manstein argued, however, that while Guderian saw only the Panzer arm, the general staff had to consider the entire army. He further argued that in contrast to the enthusiastic and impatient Guderian, the chief of the general staff could not responsibly commit the German army to revolutionary armour doctrine and organization before these were thoroughly tested and proven in exercises and manoeuvres. Indeed, Manstein pointed out, it was after all Beck who after sufficient evidence had been gathered ordered the creation of the first three Panzer divisions and combined them in strategic (*operativ*) roles in operational planning and manoeuvres.[116] Manstein's arguments have been revived, endorsed, and elaborated upon by historians since the relevant documents became available.[117]

All these are historically important points, which widen and balance the picture, but do not change it that much. Not unlike his British counterparts, Chief of the General Staff Beck was by no means inattentive and unreceptive to modern ideas, weapons, and techniques, but he was nonetheless far behind the cutting edge in the field. He was propelled forward to the length that he was by the combined pressure of two forces, one from without and one from within. The former was developments abroad, especially in the British and French armies which, as a highly professional staff officer who had the greatest respect for both armies, Beck studied most carefully. The latter was the abrasive and persistent Guderian (whom the refined Beck personally disliked), who in his constant hammering of his point shrewdly utilized the developments abroad to increase the pressure. The struggle went on until Beck's resignation, and although he implemented much of the radicals' programme, he came close to watering it down crucially throughout the period.

The German field service regulations, composed by Beck in the early 1930s and renowned for their clarity of expression and style, are a good starting-point for the development of his thought on armour. Part I (1933) is progressive in the 1918 mould, basically repeating the instructions of the previous manual (1923).[118] Tanks working in close cooperation with infantry and supported by artillery, mechanized engineers, and aircraft were to participate in the battle to break into the enemy's position with the aim of reaching its artillery zone. Part II of the manual (1934) emphasized that tanks ought to be employed at the decisive point of the battle, both in attack and defence. It repeated the instructions of Part I, but also added that tanks could be combined with other motorized troops into Panzer formations which might be employed in a more independent role against the enemy's flank or rear, or for a breakthrough. Motorized infantry and light armoured formations were also envisaged.[119] The two-sided pressure was beginning its work.

As Manstein simply put it: 'The general staff from early on envisaged the employment of large, independent Panzer formations, because of the pioneering British experiments and the writings of General Fuller and Captain Liddell Hart.'[120] We have already seen the reports composed in the general staff and those sent from London by Geyer von Schweppenburg, Beck's confidante, on the British armour manoeuvres of 1932 and 1934. Beck himself extensively studied the 1934 manoeuvres, and for a good reason. Following the creation of the British 1st Tank Brigade as a permanent formation in the spring of that year and its exercises in August in deep strategic penetration, an experimental Mobile Division had been tried out for the first time in September. The divisional exercise had been judged a failure, and Beck was therefore justified in being more reserved than some of his subordinates towards the idea of large armoured formations. But his careful analysis was unbiased, and while highlighting the problems encountered and the fact that even the widely experienced British army had found it difficult to handle large armoured formations, he left the question of their feasibility open for the time being. Furthermore, he assessed that the British would decide to proceed on their course and create a permanent mobile division.[121] The understandably cautious approach, expressed in his saying to Guderian: 'but why should *we* be the first to create them?' [Panzer divisions], thereby lost much of its ground.[122]

Beck now subjected the use of tanks to a series of trials. In June 1935 a general staff tour played out (without troops) a German counter-offensive against a Czechoslovakian offensive in the Erz Mountains. The counter-offensive was to be carried out by infantry and three (still non-existent) Panzer divisions. Given the nature of the terrain chosen, it is not surprising that Beck concluded that the Panzer force had been able to operate effectively only in limited parts of the whole area and that it was 'the weapon of good opportunity'. He wrote that in the first stage of a campaign tanks must be employed in close cooperation with the infantry formations and under their overall command to break the enemy's position and reach his artillery zone. Only when this was achieved, could Panzer formations be employed independently to exploit the success against the enemy's flank and rear or for the breakthrough. Beck therefore concluded that in addition to Panzer formations the army would need strong tank battalions and regiments to be kept in the army's reserve for cooperation with the infantry in the main battle. This was to remain his position from then on. He also expressed reservations regarding the Panzer commanders' system of forward command.[123]

At the end of August 1935 the Panzer troops were assembled for trials as an experimental Panzer division. The trials focused on the basics of command, control, and tactical handling, and in this respect stood half-way between Broad's manoeuvres with the armoured brigade in 1931 and the British 1934 manoeuvres. The report by the Command of the Panzer Troops, signed by Lutz, stressed that the division was a purely offensive instrument both in attack and defence. It envisaged two types of missions for it: an independent strategic (*operativ*) strike, launched by surprise immediately at the outbreak of war against the enemy's flank and rear; or cooperation with other formations. The report objected to the idea of giving each infantry division a tank battalion, or a regiment to each infantry corps. It maintained that this could only lead to local successes and would disperse the armour. In what appears to be a fall-back position, it proposed instead that Panzer brigades would be created to support the infantry, while Panzer divisions would be concentrated in corps for independent strategic (*operativ*) roles.[124]

Three Panzer divisions were established in October 1935, but for Beck this was only part of a general programme for the development of armour for the 'offensive army' now being created. He specified three roles for the tanks: support for the infantry attack ('infantry tanks'), fighting enemy tanks, and independent strategic (*operativ*) employment in cooperation with other motorized arms. In addition to the Panzer divisions, of which he wanted no more, he planned to create a Panzer regiment for each regular corps by September 1939, which would be concentrated in Panzer brigades. This would give 36 battalions for cooperation with infantry as against 12 in the three Panzer divisions. Beck also planned the creation of semi-motorized and motorized infantry divisions and units, and mentioned the possibility of forming light mechanized divisions.[125] In short, Beck understandably looked around and wished to do what other leading armies were doing. At exactly that time, the British announced their intention to gradually motorize their infantry divisions and provide each of them with a battalion of infantry tanks for close support, in addition to the formation of the Mobile Division. These tank battalions would be concentrated in army tank brigades. And in the summer of 1935 the French conducted large scale manoeuvres in Champagne to try out their new light mechanized division (DLM) and new motorized infantry divisions, established the year before.[126]

Beck repeatedly referred to the experience and conduct of other armies when defending his programme for a multiple role for armour against the conservative counter-proposals of the General Army Office (*Allgemeines Heeresamt*). For economic reasons, the head of the General Army Office, Colonel Fromm, claimed that infantry support was the main role of tanks, and argued that arming them with machine-guns would be largely sufficient because fighting enemy tanks should not be their role. Again outlining his programme, Beck insisted that a tank with an armour-piercing 37 mm gun had to be the backbone of the armoured force. Regarding the Panzer divisions he wrote:

> Whether the way we have taken last year in assembling a number of battalions in Panzer divisions is right or wrong, I would not yet like today to express a final judgement. I believe, however, that I can determine that the exercises conducted last summer by the Command of the Panzer Troops in the Munster Training Area, as well as the development in other countries, give a safe clue that in the formation of Panzer divisions the leading idea is not wrong.[127]

On the other side, of course, Beck's compromise solution was still very far from Guderian's insistence on avoiding any diversion of armour from the Panzer divisions.

During 1936 the general staff under Beck's direction was planning the creation of four motorized infantry divisions, to be established in 1937, and of light mechanized divisions, to be formed one each year from 1937 onward. As mentioned before, both types were initiated by Beck in imitation of the French. Both types were viewed principally as a strategic (*operativ*) weapon for mobile use, and the former in particular was largely intended for cooperation with the Panzer divisions.[128] Guderian, who would probably not have initiated the motorized infantry divisions himself, recognized their value. He totally objected, however, to the light divisions, which contained only one battalion of light tanks and were intended for 'cavalry type' missions, such as reconnaissance, screening, delaying action, exploitation of success, and pursuit. He argued that strategic reconnaissance could better be carried out by aircraft, and that none of the missions specified necessitated a special mobile division.[129] The Polish campaign proved him right, after which the light divisions were converted to Panzer. However, the main problem from Guderian's point of view was the Panzer units intended for infantry support. Until autumn 1938, after Beck's departure, no new Panzer divisions were created, and the number of tanks coming from new production and remaining out of these divisions was progressively outweighing those in the divisions. Two independent Panzer brigades were created, and more were planned. It has been claimed that Beck simply wanted to keep an open mind and all the options open until more practical experience was gained.[130] Indeed ultimately, when the German army so decided, it did not find it difficult to concentrate all its armour in new Panzer divisions. Still, Beck's decisions cannot be explained away so easily. In the first place his view regarding the multiple role of armour was principled and firm. Moreover, in 1936 he insisted on the production of a special, heavily armoured 'infantry tank' in addition to the main battle tank and fire-support tank (Panzer III and IV), ordered in 1935 and 1934 respectively.

A general staff document, issued by the organization branch but exactly repeating the views expressed by Guderian in an article he had written at that time, argued against Beck's request that in view of the strength of the modern anti-tank gun, heavily armoured infantry tanks would not be effective. The document suggested that it was better to concentrate all tanks in armoured divisions for strategic (*operativ*) use. It also argued that because of industrial shortages the infantry tank would not be available in less than four to five years.[131] Nonetheless, by late 1936 Beck ordered the work on the infantry tank to go on.[132] The documentary record appears to break off at the end of that year, and it is therefore not exactly clear how the matter ended. Possibly the idea of infantry tanks was ultimately given up in favour of self-propelled artillery (*Sturmartillerie*), belonging to the artillery and intended for the infantry divisions. The first of these weapons were beginning to come off production in 1940. Their value, especially under conditions of scarcity in resources for armour and as they were intended for the non-motorized infantry, was hotly contested between Guderian and Manstein both before and after the war.[133] The point, however, is that had Beck had his way and the production of a large number of heavily armoured infantry tanks been taken up, this would have created the sort of divergence in tanks' mobility that was to hinder the concentrated use of the Allies' numerically superior armour in 1940, and continued to plague the British army throughout the war. In the same way that in his decision to create the first Panzer divisions in 1935 Beck was following on the British pioneering model, he wanted to stay in line with developments abroad at the time that British tank policy itself was changing and was about to come closer to the French pattern with the decision by Elles and Martel to drop the old universal 'medium' design in favour of the differentiated 'infantry' and 'cruiser' types.[134]

From all this it can be seen that, as in other countries, 'reactionaries' in regards to armour were a minority in the German army and general staff. By and large, the general staffs in practically all armies were dominated by 'mildly conservative' to 'progressive' officers who recognized very well the value of the tank and wanted to use it in large numbers for a variety of roles.[135] Beck, too, belonged to this category. Yet, however understandable the mainstream attitude of not placing all the eggs in one basket may appear, the future belonged to the 'radical' programme which insisted on concentrating the tanks in armoured formations and opposed their being tied down to foot walking infantry. The significance of these diverging concepts should not be underrated. For the Germans, and probably also for the other powers, this was very much the source of the difference between triumph and disaster in 1939–41. Later on in the war, when all armies learnt to handle and confront armour, tanks would again have to cooperate closely with the infantry for the break in battle. But creating a special type of infantry tank, attached to and designed to support non-motorized infantry, was never to prove a good idea.

This is also the principal theoretical factor explaining the attitude of the creators of the German Panzer arm to Soviet armour and the doctrine of 'deep battle'. The Germans possessed a comprehensive and accurate picture of the new Soviet theories, a picture which was as good as that which the West would ever have before the opening of the Soviet archives. Ostensibly the information was derived from analysing Soviet military literature, but the cooperation with the Soviets in 1928–33 may have given the Germans a closer insight. In 1932 a comprehensive article, 'The Tactical and Strategic (*operativ*) Employment of Modern Tanks in the Red Army', was published in *Militär-Wochenblatt*. It presented the theory of deep battle with its various complementary parts and corresponding tank types and tank missions. Light tanks would be used for reconnaissance and pursuit, heavy and infantry-support tanks for the break in, and medium tanks for deep penetrations to destroy enemy artillery, reserves, command posts, and the like. The latter category of armour would be organized in mechanized formations of up to one thousand tanks and would operate up to a depth of 200–300 km and along a similar width. It was reported that the Soviets were planning to create a 15,000 strong tank force, of which about half would participate in a general offensive.[136] More surveys were published in the journal in the following years. In 1934 Major Walter Nehring described the new Soviet advances in his book on armour. He wrote that the Russians were fast developing tanks, borrowing extensively from abroad, but increasingly gaining dividends from their own growing tractor and track industry. They already possessed an estimated 1200 tanks and were creating many 'motor-mechanized' brigades, divided between long-distance groups (*Fernwirkungsgruppe*), long-distance infantry support groups (*Fernunterstützungsgruppe*), and close infantry support groups (*Nahunterstützungsgruppe*), intended for operation in various depths.[137] In 1935 the new edition of Heigl's *Pocket Book of Tanks* also stressed Soviet Russia's great advances in tank production during the previous three years. The book stated that Soviet armour doctrine stood halfway between the British and the French, dividing the tanks as it did between long-distance and infantry support groups, with the former intended for deep strikes in a Fullerite fashion to destroy the enemy's nervous system.[138]

In 1935 works by two Soviet writers on deep battle, Kryshanowski and Kriwoschein, were translated into German. The first of these was the more general and stressed the doctrine's emphasis on the simultaneous attack at all levels and in all depths in order to effect a complete disintegration and total destruction of the enemy's army. The mechanized independent long-distance groups would strike immediately to a depth of at least 50 and up to 150 km at the army level, and of 100–200 km at the front level. The structures of Soviet armoured and mechanized brigades were appended to the book.[139] Internal general staff reports portrayed the same picture.[140] The Soviet 1936 large-scale manoeuvres, which impressed foreign observers with their modern and combined use of armour, aircraft, and paratroopers, were extensively covered by *Militär-Wochenblatt*.[141] Finally, a comprehensive summary of the concept of deep battle, both in attack and defence, reflecting the stage reached in the Soviet Field Service Regulations of 1936 (PU 36), was published in the general staff's journal.[142]

Guderian, too, was fully cognizant and respectful of the massive nature of Soviet Russia's industrialization and of the Red Army's mechanization. He visited the Soviet Union with Lutz in 1932, during the period of German–Soviet cooperation, and was much impressed by its tank production.[143] Like Nehring, he produced the data gathered by German intelligence and at the disposal of the Command of the Panzer Troops. With 10,000 tanks, 150,000 tractors, and 100,000 other vehicles, he wrote, 'the Red Army was ahead of all armies in mechanization, leaving Britain and France far behind'. He, too, described the concept of deep battle and the three armour group types, each with its special mission.[144] But this division of roles was exactly the thing he and his friends objected to. Like all foreign observers (such as the British Lieutenant-Colonel Martel), the Germans probably assessed that there was a wide gap between the enormity of Soviet Russia's armament programme and its sophisticated military doctrine on the one hand and the effectiveness of its actual battlefield performance on the other. Having only shortly before been the Soviets' mentors, they were accustomed to regard the Red Army as half-backward. The conservative Beck, for example, looked only to the two West European powers, even though the Red Army's armour theory and practice could be enlisted to support his views. The younger officers of the Panzer arm were less prejudiced, but it was the theory itself that they rejected. After describing the various Soviet armour group types, Nehring concluded that the permanent functional splitting of armour in that fashion was schematic and inflexible. Guderian wrote that while 'there is something to be said' for it, it 'demands a whole inventory of specialized tanks, with all the attendant disadvantages'. While he maintained that the Russians were leading in mechanization, Guderian held a different model of armour doctrine and organization. He described three main variants in the world's armies regarding the employment of armour. In France the tanks belonged to the infantry and were also used in cavalry-type missions. 'Russia has advanced the farthest' in a second direction: using armour for infantry support as well as independently. However, 'the British since the war have taken a different route from the Russians and the French'. Their armour had been freed from cooperation with foot walking infantry. And it was to this direction that Guderian so strongly adhered.[145]

Although by then Guderian was of course well aware that the British themselves no longer strictly adhered to the model described, the 'British way' in the employment of armour had long become a symbol and the name of a generic type. Furthermore, for at least two years after the creation of the first Panzer divisions, Hobart's manoeuvres with the 1st Tank Brigade, in which long-range strategic penetrations were tried out, continued as before to be the focus of attention for the creators of the Panzer arm. It is important to realize that in those years the Germans, like the British in earlier years, were mainly preoccupied with the basics of organization, tactics, and, not least, the development of a workable system of radio communication, without which no far-flung operations could be seriously contemplated.[146] As mentioned before, the inaugural manoeuvres of 1935 were of a rudimentary nature, and the armour enthusiasts were frustrated by the fact that no large-scale armoured manoeuvres took place in 1936. The first were held only in the autumn of 1937 when the 3rd Panzer Division and 1st Panzer Brigade of the 1st Panzer Division (800 tanks in all) took part in the great Wehrmacht manoeuvres across north Germany, in the presence of many distinguished foreign guests, including the much impressed British CIGS, Field-Marshal Sir Cyril Deverell.[147] It was only from that time on, not before, that the German Panzer force, still suffering from teething problems and lacking its planned war equipment (only the light Panzer I was in service), took a definite lead in the field of armoured warfare. From about that time it was also beginning to profit from its experience in the Spanish Civil War, especially in respect to the practicalities of air–ground cooperation.[148] Hitherto, in the years 1934–36, the Germans had still been eagerly watching the British armour manoeuvres.

Unfortunately, the surviving official German records on the subject for the immediate prewar years appear to be particularly thin. For example, only one file, containing the mainly political reports, seems to have survived from the dispatches sent by Geyer and by his successor from London in the years 1936–38.[149] The intelligence files on the world's armies also provide a patchy picture.[150] Only the open publications give a better one. The British manoeuvres of 1936, including those of the Tank Brigade, were reviewed by *Militär-Wochenblatt*. It was reported that the brigade (200 tanks) exercised in tank vs. tank warfare. Also, 'the marching exercises were nearly always so laid out that they would go far around the enemy's wing, and the armoured brigade would then strike at his flank'.[151] The *Militär-Wochenblatt's* review of the brigade's manoeuvres in 1937 was based specifically on Liddell Hart's report in *The Times*. His emphasis on supplying the brigade from the air and off the land in which it was operating was cited.[152] Indeed it was from this period that Liddell Hart would later receive a distant echo of the British and of his own influence on the development of German armour, which for years would remain his most significant one.

In 1941 Liddell Hart suddenly received a letter from the wife of a tank officer who in 1939 had been staying at the Bulgarian officers' club in Pleven. There she met Colonel Khandyeff, a Bulgarian officer who had been attached to a German armoured division a few years earlier. She described his recollection of his experience in these words:

> The divisional commander was absolutely mad about the exploited and unexploited possibilities of tanks. His faith in armoured formations was such that he took a tremendous amount of pain in planting the same enthusiasm in the people under him.
>
> He spent his own money on providing copies of foreign books and periodicals, as well as on the services of a local tutor for the rough translations. His gods were General Fuller and Captain Liddell Hart. Liddell Hart, he considered, was the best analytical brain in the world, and his articles translated, read and studied, were discussed long before they would be vetted and sent from Berlin.
>
> While with him, Liddell Hart's accounts of the manoeuvres began to appear in *The Times*. As much as possible, every move of the manoeuvres was copied and put into practical demonstration. It was like a rehearsal of a play. The General was the happiest and busiest man, saying that Hobart gave him an answer to so many queries – and an inspiration. When a visiting anti-tank expert spoke of tank limitations as well as tank or no-tank country, quoting various opinions, including those of well-known people in England, the General impatiently dismissed him by saying – 'It is the old school, and already old history. I put my faith in Hobart, in the new man'.[153]

After the war, in 1945, General Wilhelm von Thoma, who had been one of the leading officers in the German Panzer arm since its inception, told Liddell Hart that he remembered the visit of the Bulgarian colonel and that he thought the general referred to was Guderian. He confirmed that the Germans had been keenly studying British military writings and had been closely watching the manoeuvres of the British armoured brigade in its successive forms. Guderian, when asked about the Bulgarian colonel's story by a fellow German general *before* Liddell Hart made direct contact with him, replied that he was not sure that it was his division that the Bulgarian colonel had referred to but that it very well may have been: 'It is however certain that I had read many articles by Liddell Hart and that they were always of burning interest to me and that I have learnt much from them.' In response to Liddell Hart's direct inquiry in his first letter to him, Guderian clarified the point as follows: 'I don't remember him being present at the manoeuvres of my Panzer division. But as Thoma remembered meeting him and I was Thoma's divisional commander at the time, I think that Khandyeff was speaking about me in his letter.' After further urging by Liddell Hart he wrote: 'The account of Colonel Khandyeff referred to 1935–6, when I was in command of the 2nd Panzer Division at Wurzburg.'[154] The later year was probably the correct one, first, because the German Panzer divisions were created only on 15 October 1935, whereas Hobart's exercises of that year had been held, as usual, in August; and second, because Guderian was promoted from colonel to major-general only on 1 August 1936.

This telling episode squares perfectly with what we have been seeing all along. Although in response to later inquiries Guderian informed Liddell Hart that before the war he had read his *When Britain Goes to War*, *The Future of Infantry*, and *The Remaking of Modern Armies*,[155] it appears that it had been primarily Liddell Hart's *articles* that he had been following with 'burning interest' and from which he had been 'learning much'. We have seen that Mearsheimer missed the bulk of Liddell Hart's writings on armoured warfare, published chiefly in his columns in *The Daily Telegraph* and *The Times* rather than in his books and magazine articles. He therefore claimed that Liddell Hart had written very little about the theory of armoured warfare; had ceased almost entirely to write about and argue for it in the 1930s; and above all had never advocated deep strategic penetration before the Second World War. It is now clear, however, that Liddell Hart's later comment, which Mearsheimer cites with ridicule as patently evasive, was in fact entirely true; in 1953 Liddell Hart wrote that the adoption of his ideas on the expanding torrent in tank doctrine, 'both here and in Germany ... was produced not from any one exposition of it in a book, but rather by a constant reiteration of the keynote in my current articles commenting on manoeuvres etc.'[156]

All this also helps to explain another fact which has recently come to the attention of scholars and has greatly impressed them. Kenneth Macksey has pointed out that the bibliography to Guderian's *Achtung Panzer!* (1937) cites no work by Liddell Hart, even though he is mentioned in the text, whereas it does include books by Swinton, Fuller, Martel, and even de Gaulle. Macksey has interpreted this as proof that Liddell Hart's influence on Guderian was much more limited than the former boasted.[157] However, once we realize that Liddell Hart's main contribution to the theory of armoured warfare and to the creators of the Panzer arm was made in his articles, a fact of which at least Macksey seems to be aware,[158] the picture looks different. *Achtung Panzer!* was a collection of Guderian's lectures and articles, published to popularize the Panzer arm with the general public. The attached bibliography was in fact a small elementary source list [*Quellenverzeichnis*]. More than half of the book was dedicated to tanks in the First World War, and so were about half of the entries in the source list. Only one book each was cited for Fuller, Swinton and Martel, and in each case this book was in fact the record of their personal service with the tanks.[159] Liddell Hart had no comparable book, though had his *When Britain Goes to War* already existed in a German translation (translated the same year *Achtung Panzer!* was published), it probably would have been included in the source list. There was little point in referring readers to his scattered articles in *The Daily Telegraph* and *The Times*. Finally, there were the limits in which *Achtung Panzer!* was written. The sub-title of the book was 'The Development of Armoured Forces, Their Tactics and Operational [*operativ*] Potential', and in the text Guderian mentioned that 'the tank forces would gain by [the British way of employing them] not only a local, tactical importance on the battlefield, but one which extended into the operational [*operativ*] sphere of the theatre of war as a whole'.[160] Still, as Macksey has noted, 'the latest thoughts about the ambitious role of Panzer divisions for deep penetration were muted' in the book.[161] And it was there that Liddell Hart's main contribution lay.

There is a related point which the episode of the Bulgarian colonel may illustrate. Guderian was using Liddell Hart's reports of the manoeuvres of the British Tank Brigade as a major source of information. He thought highly of him both as a theorist of armoured warfare and as a military critic. He was undoubtedly well aware of Liddell Hart's habit of using his reports to advance his own views. Nonetheless, he could not have known of the close cooperation, the virtual unanimity, and the stimulating exchange of ideas which existed between Liddell Hart and Hobart. In short, he could not have been fully aware of the degree to which Liddell Hart, through his partnership with Hobart during the period 1933–37 in which deep penetrations by armoured formations were actually put into practice in Britain, was directly involved in, and contributing to, the advancement of his favourite idea. This went beyond Fuller's pioneering conceptions which had never progressed after having been last codified in *Lectures on FSR III* (1932).

After the middle of the 1930s the fame of Fuller and Liddell Hart reached new heights in Germany. The first reason for this was that now their books and not only their articles were being translated and published, rather than being merely abstracted, serialized, and reviewed in German professional journals. The list of Liddell Hart's books translated before the war included: *The Future of Infantry* (1934), *Lawrence* (1935), *When Britain Goes to War* (1937), *Scipio* (1938), *Foch* (1938), and *The Defence of Britain* (1939). The equivalent list for Fuller included: *Generalship* (1935), *Memoirs* (1939), and *The First of the League Wars* (1939). There is little doubt that Fuller kept his more senior place as the founding father of 'modern' armoured warfare and of the 'British school'. He was treated as such by all experts. He undoubtedly also held the senior place among Guderian's 'gods' throughout the interwar years. Fuller never actively searched for accolades after the Second World War but, as the British military attaché in Berlin in 1939, Brigadier T. Denis Daly, recalled: 'General Guderian ... told me at length of his studies of the writings of Major-Gen. Fuller.'[162] In addition to everything else, Fuller was a fascist, and his political and politically charged writings were prominently cited in Germany. He visited Germany several times during the Nazi period as an official guest, was received with great honour, and met among others with Hitler, Ribbentrop, and Hess.[163] Guderian's elder son has written in reply to Macksey's inquiries:

> As far as I know it was Fuller who made the most suggestions. Once before the war my father visited him. Fuller was certainly more competent as an active officer than Captain B.H. Liddell Hart.... At any rate my father often spoke of him while I cannot remember other names being mentioned at that time.... The greater emphasis upon Liddell Hart seems to have developed through contacts after the war.[164]

No matter how exactly this evidence is interpreted,[165] it was in fact mainly to Hobart, with Liddell Hart behind him, that Guderian's attention was turned in the years 1934–37. For while Fuller remained the giant figurehead of armoured theory, armoured warfare during the mid-1930s was being rapidly developed by real fighting formations on the plains of southern England.

Another factor that greatly enhanced Liddell Hart's fame in Germany in the second half of the 1930s was the fact that he was now writing for *The Times*. Even more than before, he was now by far the most frequently cited foreign strategic authority – from Britain or from any other country – appearing in nearly every weekly issue of *Militär-Wochenblatt* over some years and always referred to with the greatest respect. Among other things, his latest operational precepts were cited in the German journals practically every time they appeared in English. These forecasted the growing strength of defence owing to the growing number of anti-tank weapons and the defender's increasing ability to rush up mobile reserves to block the attacker's breakthroughs; but they also proposed methods which armies and armoured formations might use under the changing conditions. Most importantly, where Liddell Hart suggested the best chances of armoured formations lay:

> One must use the rapidity of deep penetrating leverage to demoralize the enemy by creating repeated flanking threats which he would be unable to parry. One must advance on a wide front in order to be able to envelop the enemy and find and penetrate through gaps in his front. For that purpose it is best to advance on as many roads and with as many spearheads as possible, thus improving the chances of locating an 'inner flank'.

This is the method termed 'the expanding torrent', in which 'every subordinate commander should penetrate as deep as possible', and the reserves follow in order to support and exploit successes.[166]

Having already seen a great deal of the evidence for the decisiveness of British influence on the formation of the Panzer arm and the development of its characteristic doctrine, it is time to pause for a more general question, of a theoretical as well as practical significance. Liddell Hart's conception of the 'indirect approach' aimed (in Fuller's spirit) at disorienting, dislocating, and causing the disintegration of the enemy by a variety of means other than battle. Much of this was assimilated into British armour doctrine during the 1920s and 1930s. By contrast, was not the German 'Blitzkrieg', while employing revolutionary new weapons and techniques, in fact combat-oriented and aimed at great battles of encirclement and annihilation (*Kesselschlachten*), in line with traditional Prussian–German doctrine against which Liddell Hart had crystallized his ideas in the first place?[167] After all, Guderian's favourite slogan was 'boot 'em, don't spatter 'em' [*Klotzen, nicht Kleckern*].[168]

To clarify this point one must turn to the famous concept of 'Blitzkrieg'. It is an incredible and seemingly inexplicable historiographical fact that it has taken nearly fifty years after the Second World War for the realization slowly to filter through that, contrary to widely held perceptions, 'Blitzkrieg' was not the name of any official or at first even unofficial German doctrine allegedly crystallized during the interwar period.[169] It was a popular foreign designation invented outside Germany following her first swift victories in the Second World War. Liddell Hart, who referred to the German 'Blitzkrieg' and 'lightning war' in 1939, even before the war, and later implied that he had invented the concept, was apparently not the only media man to have used the phrase. In July 1940 *Militär-Wochenblatt* wrote that the term Blitzkrieg 'stemmed from the ranks of our adversaries and quickly went into currency also with us'. Guderian wrote similarly in his memoirs: 'as a result of the successes of our rapid campaigns our enemies coined the word Blitzkrieg'.[170]

Being an undefined and retrospective concept, 'Blitzkrieg' could be, and has been, given various and often arbitrary interpretations which regarded it as Germany's preplanned strategy – politically, economically, and militarily.[171] The fact that no such overall official doctrine existed does not, however, mean that what came to be known as 'Blitzkrieg' at the beginning of the Second World War did not rest on real developments and strategic ideas in pre-war Germany. Militarily, what the Germans had before the war was first their traditional strategic doctrine, embodied in the latest edition of their field service regulations (composed by Beck in 1933–34) but stretching back to the era of Napoleon, the Prussian reformers, and the Wars of Unification. This doctrine emphasized *inter alia* vigorous and offensive action in order to destroy the enemy's armed forces in great battles. The lessons of the First World War, while highlighting the need for total economic and social mobilization for a protracted war, also added new urgency to the traditional imperative of achieving a rapid decision, so that an attrition war against a superior enemy coalition could be averted. Thus, much of the confusion generated by the debate on whether German political, economic, and military planners postulated total mobilization predicated on *Volksgemeinschaft* or desired short and swift coups is in fact out of place. *Both* notions were there, and were regarded more as complementary than as conflicting. Since Germany was fundamentally weaker than her combined enemies, she had to mobilize her resources to the utmost *as well as* do everything she could to win unconventionally and avoid attrition. As early as 28 February

1934, addressing army and SA leaders at the Reichswehr ministry, Hitler predicted that in order to gain living space in the east for the German people in the teeth of international opposition, 'short, decisive blows to the West and then to the East could be necessary'.[172] Both Hitler and the armed forces' high command promoted the air and mechanized forces as instruments for that purpose, and each of these forces had its own operational doctrine. 'Blitzkrieg' evolved in stages in Poland and France as all these factors unravelled and interacted in the political and strategic circumstances created during the first phase of the Second World War. It embodied many inherent tensions, reflecting Germany's fundamental material weaknesses as well as diverging operational concepts within her high command.

Now let us return to the evolution of pre-war German armour doctrine. From its inception the Panzer arm adopted a mode of operation which was influenced by British theory which had served as its model. This mode was described as follows in a German news-sheet disseminated at the end of 1933 and dealing with the employment of the armoured formation:

> The manner of its engagement is not in prolonged battles but short, well-timed operations launched by brief orders. The principle is to use the battle tanks at the core of operations, to concentrate the main fighting force at the decisive point of action ... on the principle of surprise in order to avoid or avert enemy defensive action.[173]

British armour doctrine, Lieutenant-Colonel Nehring of the Panzer arm wrote with approval, stressed rapid hammer blows rather than drawn-out battles.[174]

Of course, Guderian and his friends wanted to employ the Panzer formations for achieving crushing military decisions, sometimes by means of great encirclement battles. Yet they also had a more far-reaching conception regarding the manner by which decisive results could be brought about. As is well known, during the major 'Blitzkrieg' campaigns in the West and in Russia, intense disputes developed within the German high command regarding the pattern and aim of operations. The commanders of the infantry armies, more conservative in outlook and fearing, or struggling with, stiff enemy resistance along the fronts and flanks penetrated by the Panzer forces, wanted these forces to assist in ringing the enemy's armies in order to effect great *Kesselschlachten*. On the other side, the Panzer leaders, most notably Guderian, resisted this request and saw the role of the mechanized forces as driving as deep and as fast as possible into the enemy's territory with the view of bringing about a total collapse of his armed resistance and getting hold of his main communications and civilian centres.[175] Whether this was possible, especially in the Russian campaign in which enemy resistance was much more stubborn than that which the Germans had experienced in the West and where spaces were many times more vast, is another matter. The idea, however, was that conducting or even winning 'ordinary' battles would only slow down the German offensive, cause the attrition of the Panzer force, and leave the enemy time to recover. Indeed, at least in the West in 1940, the most successful 'Blitzkrieg' of them all, victory was gained 'strategically', with the Allies taken completely off balance, and hence with remarkably little hard fighting.

Moving to another, related question: both classical German doctrine and Liddell Hart were agreed in advocating calculated wide dispersion, changing into rapid concentrations; but was not 'Blitzkrieg' in fact based on massive knife-like concentrations of mechanized troops on narrow fronts? Critics of the conduct of British armour in the early North African campaigns have pointed out the tendency of the British commanders to spread their forces excessively widely, thus exposing them to the concentrated blows of the German Afrika Korps. Although Liddell Hart always insisted that dispersion must be calculated so as to enable effective cooperation, mutual support, and rapid concentration, it has been claimed with some justice that British armoured thinking during the 1930s, very much under his influence, emphasized very wide dispersion as the normal pattern of armoured operations.[176] Obviously, the balance between 'calculated dispersion' and 'rapid concentration' can be interpreted very differently in practice. Interestingly, in February 1942 *Militär-Wochenblatt* cited Liddell Hart's criticism in *The Daily Mail* of British handling of armour in North Africa. The problem, he wrote, was that the British used their armour piecemeal, whereas Rommel concentrated his.[177] Historically more significant, however, was the fact that German armour doctrine was itself similar to the British, from which indeed it had been derived.

The British armour's principle of advancing on a wide front, noted for example in Beck's study of the 1934 manoeuvres,[178] was well-recognized and accepted without question by the creators of the Panzer arm.[179] Consider for instance the most informative and programmatic of Guderian articles, published in 1939, where he wrote as follows: 'The success of an offensive will increase the wider the front and the greater the depth on which it is conducted.' Guderian claimed that breakthroughs on narrow fronts would especially expose the unarmoured tail of the armoured formations to enemy flanking fire. In addition, only on wide fronts would it be possible to employ several Panzer divisions together.[180] Well into the war in 1940 a German armour manual prescribed that decision should be attained by means of rapid concentration and deep penetration on wide fronts.[181] German and British conduct may have differed in reality during the war, but their respective doctrines were similar.

Naturally, there have been other claims of influence on the formation and doctrine of the Panzer divisions. Liddell Hart was deeply stung when Churchill told Parliament in 1942 that the Germans were implementing the ideas first formulated by de Gaulle, now leader of the Free French. For years Liddell Hart agonized about this rival claim, until he was able to solicit the support of the German generals against it. The evidence of the 1930s themselves show that de Gaulle's *Vers l'armée de métier* (1934) received considerable attention in Germany and was translated in 1935. The book and the author were prominently cited by the German armour pioneers, together with the names of other French advocates of mechanization like Generals Alléhaud and Camon. All were presented in the propaganda campaign within the German army as the 'progressive' school in the French army.[182] Nonetheless, the veterans of the Panzer arm told Liddell Hart after the war that by the time de Gaulle's book had been published their own minds had long been made up and that his proposals had anyhow been much too impressionistic and hazy to be of practical use. In view of the substance of de Gaulle's book and of what we know about the development of the idea of armoured warfare in Germany, this testimony seems flawless. Furthermore, de Gaulle, who dwarfed even Liddell Hart in egocentrism and vanity, made no reference in his book to his French predecessors, let alone, as Liddell Hart complained, to the British school. But in 1943, in reply to a question about his book he said: 'But what about your best soldier, General Fuller? He was the prophet, we only followed him.... You will find prophesied in his books everything that the Germans did with tanks.'[183]

A more serious claim for influence belongs to the Austrian reserve artillery general, Ludwig Ritter von Eimannsberger. His book *Tank War* (1934; second edn. 1938) started with a survey of the history of armour during and after the First World War. He contrasted the French and British armour philosophies, describing the British pioneering manoeuvres from 1927 on and citing Fuller's ideas advocating tank fleets and an independent strategic (*operativ*) employment of armour. Whether strategic penetration was possible, he wrote, was a question which in his own opinion still remained open; the British believed that it was.[184] Eimannsberger then outlined a prophetic blueprint for the use of armoured and motorized divisions both in reserve for counter-offensives within the framework of defence in depth and for the attack.[185] Playing out a fictitious new Battle of Amiens, he projected a three-stage affair: first the enemy defensive lines would be penetrated in cooperation with armour; then the enemy's tank reserves would be defeated; and finally armoured and mechanized divisions would exploit the success independently.[186] Probably the most interesting part of Eimannsberger's book was his proposals for the structure of the armoured and motorized divisions, which were fairly similar to those actually adopted by the German army in the following years. He also proposed tank brigades for the role of infantry close support.[187] It is difficult to know how influential Eimannsberger actually was. His book was widely known in professional circles in Germany, and after its publication he contributed regularly and prominently on armour to German military journals. Yet the officers of the Panzer arm denied that he had any significant influence, claiming that he merely reinforced already existing thoughts and plans.[188] Perhaps the nature of his proposals suggests some influence on Beck in the very period the latter was struggling to make up his mind on the question of mechanized forces. In any case, Eimannsberger dropped his doubts regarding the strategic use of armour only in the late 1930s and in the second edition of his book, and repeatedly pointed to Britain as his authoritative model.[189]

Indeed later divergences during the Second World War have obscured the degree to which the creators of the Panzer divisions in the mid-1930s based themselves on the British model in almost everything they did. The first German Panzer manoeuvres copied the tactical problems of the British exercises.[190] The British principle of mixing light and medium companies in the tank battalions was adopted by the Germans and was not abandoned before the end of the Second World War.[191] Moreover, the structure of the Panzer division itself was modelled on the British. Critics and historians of British armour have focused on the conflict between Lindsay and Hobart in 1934 regarding the structure of the mobile division and have described the later development on the eve of the Second World War of the tank-heavy British armoured division which contained very little infantry and not enough of the supporting arms. But for the creators of the Panzer arm in the mid-1930s all these were unknown and insignificant. What mattered for them was what was actually taking place at the time on Salisbury Plains. All German reports of the 1934 manoeuvres of the experimental mobile division emphasized that this time the Tank Brigade (four battalions strong) cooperated within a single divisional structure with a motorized infantry brigade, motorized artillery, and motorized elements of reconnaissance, engineers and signals.[192] This exactly was the structure adopted for the first Panzer divisions in 1935. The British continued to debate the structure of the Mobile Division throughout the second half of the 1930s, and the German kept track of the debate. But the Mobile Division itself made its debut with little infantry and supporting arms only towards the beginning of the war, by which time the Germans no longer needed to look up to anybody.

Furthermore, even in theory there was little difference between the British and the Germans. Like the British theorists Fuller, Martel, and Liddell Hart, whom he cites in this context in *Achtung Panzer!*,[193] Guderian from the late 1920s had come to advocate all-arm Panzer divisions, with all their elements armoured and mounted on cross-country vehicles. At the same time, like Fuller and his disciples, the exponents of armour in Germany emphasized the leading role of the tank in the division and tended at first to relegate the infantry mainly to the second echelon of the division. The tank, read a German newssheet in 1933, 'is less well equipped to hold captured territory; for this purpose it is usually necessary to employ motorized infantry and artillery'.[194] Hence again the two separate brigade structures for the tanks and infantry in the Panzer divisions, which would be improvised into makeshift combined 'battle groups' only later in the war. To be sure, in practice, from their first exercises the German Panzer arm embraced close inter-arm cooperation and did not restrict the motorized infantry of the Panzer divisions to defensive missions only. Liddell Hart would later claim that in this the Germans were following his own teachings, and it is interesting to note that from the start summaries of his works in German journals did in fact consistently and clearly cite his concept of offensive armoured infantry or 'tank marines'.[195] His book *The Future of Infantry*, his first to be translated into German (1934), enjoyed great success in the Wehrmacht, though it must be said that it did not deal in any significant way with the infantry in the armoured division.[196] All the same, Liddell Hart's writings were far from being the decisive factor influencing German development in this respect. What mattered most was the Reichswehr's traditionally strong emphasis on inter-arm cooperation, highlighted in its service manuals, followed in practice, and taken up by the Panzer arm.[197] Liddell Hart's negative response to the inclusion of a whole motorized infantry brigade in the British mobile division of 1934 and his idea that the division needed only a handful of fully mechanized armoured infantry were noted by, but left no mark on, the Germans.[198] Unlike the British armour theorists, Guderian was grudgingly obliged to accept the fact that present resources and limited industrial capacity would not permit the provision of cross-country armoured vehicles to all the elements of the armoured division.[199] It was in all these, rather than in any principled difference of theory, that the reason for the later divergence between German and British armour lay.

Indeed, like all British armour pioneers, the creators of the Panzer arm held that the armoured division ought to be tank-heavy – the first Panzer division included 561 tanks. As in the British case, this number was almost halved by the time of the war, as medium tanks were replacing the earlier, lighter models.[200] However, as the number of tanks in the armoured division continued to decrease during the Second World War, both Guderian and Liddell Hart firmly objected to the change in their respective countries. Furthermore, the former is on the record as enlisting the latter's authority in campaigning against the reduction at the highest levels of the Wehrmacht.

After the German victory in the West and in preparation for the invasion of Russia in 1941 the number of Panzer divisions had been doubled from ten to twenty. However, low tank production had forced the reduction of the tank establishment in each division from 220–320 to 150–200, whereas the other elements in the division remained unchanged or had even been reinforced. The terrific losses sustained in the war in the east further eroded the tank establishment of the Panzer divisions, and many of them comprised no more than a few scores of tanks. Some of the younger German field commanders thought the reduction in the number of tanks in the Panzer division in fact suited the changing conditions of warfare on the Eastern Front, where forces were now even, where spectacular tank drives were no longer feasible, and where closer co-operation between the tanks and the other elements in the Panzer division had become more necessary.[201] The British and Americans, who in 1942 imitated what the Germans had done out of expediency, would reach the same conclusion in their own theatres of war. Yet most of the armoured pioneers of the interwar period thought differently. As mentioned earlier, when Guderian was nominated Inspector General of Armoured Troops after Stalingrad one of his main objectives was to bring the tank strength of the Panzer division back to its 1938 level of 400 tanks, even if that meant a reduction in the overall number of armoured divisions. To be battle-effective, he explained in a meeting with Hitler and senior staff officers on 9 March 1943, the Panzer divisions had to be very strong in tanks. Otherwise, their 'large quantity of wheeled vehicles, fuel, and personnel ... is quite disproportionate to their effectiveness'. To support his point Guderian read out to Hitler and the attending officers a recently published article by Liddell Hart on the organisation of armoured forces – past and present.[202]

This incident, not cited by historians, illustrates the point that Guderian was keeping track of Liddell Hart's writings even during the war. Indeed it will be remembered that the most solid piece of evidence for the Liddell Hart–Rommel 'connection' is also a specific comment by Rommel in the spring of 1942 on an article Liddell Hart had written on the recent campaign in the Western Desert.[203] Monitoring open enemy sources is one of the most elementary functions of any intelligence service, and German intelligence was obviously distributing the material to interested parties in the German army. Furthermore, not only German confidential reports but also the open *Militär-Wochenblatt* continued its years-old habit of printing what the two famous British military critics were writing. In 1941 Liddell Hart, who had left *The Times* in 1939, again began to write regularly on the war for the *Daily Mail*, and Fuller also was writing for a number of newspapers. From summer 1941 their commentaries on the war, especially Liddell Hart's, were cited weekly in *Militär-Wochenblatt*. The journal ran a regular section, 'Wehrpolitische Rundschau', where Liddell Hart and Fuller figured prominently as virtually the sole enemy writers to be cited side by side with Churchill, Eden, and other British cabinet ministers. As before, they remained household names in Germany. Of course, there was now an additional reason for their popularity in that country: both held pessimistic views about Britain's prospects of 'winning the war' against Germany.[204] Thus by late 1942, as it was becoming clearer that the war was not going in Germany's favour, citations in *Militär-Wochenblatt* from foreign journals and specifically from Liddell Hart and Fuller began to dwindle.

Conclusion

The idea of mechanized warfare, which centred on the tank, supported by the other arms mounted on cross-country armoured vehicles, and working in cooperation with aircraft, was pioneered in Britain from the early 1920s. Its leading proponent by far, both within the army and in public, was Fuller who by the end of the Great War had already begun to synthesize and develop with his great imaginative and historical sweep Martel's seminal notions of tank armies and the experience the British had been accumulating with the medium tank. In 1922 he converted Liddell Hart to his vision. The latter, at first only paraphrasing his master, introduced only one slight modification in that vision. Whereas Fuller and the rest of the British advocates of armour who followed in his footsteps envisaged only a defensive, 'pivot', role for the infantry in the armoured formation, Liddell Hart suggested that a small offensive element of infantry was needed to support the tanks. This, however, was much less significant than he would later make it to be, for all the armour enthusiasts agreed that the armoured formation had to be tank-heavy, with only Lindsay on the record for proposing a more balanced team in 1933–34.

It was very much owing to the propagandist efforts of Fuller and Liddell Hart, from 1925 the military correspondent of *The Daily Telegraph*, that in 1927 the British army created and tried out the world's first independent mechanized formation, employing the world's first operational long-range and fast tank, the Vickers Medium. For a decade this force and its successors would be the centre of attention and a source of inspiration for all students of mechanization in the world's leading armies. From around 1927, in connection with the trials of the experimental force, Liddell Hart began to stress the idea of long-range strategic armoured operations, driving deep into the enemy's rear to create disorientation and collapse. Here, too, he was building on Fuller's idea of penetration and paralysis, which he had adopted earlier in the 1920s; except that now he was developing it even more radically both in regard to the art of war in general in his *Strategy of Indirect Approach* and *Sherman*, and in respect to armoured warfare, mainly in his *Daily Telegraph* columns. Whereas Fuller retired from active involvement in the field of armoured warfare in the early 1930s and moved on to other interests and preoccupations, Liddell

Hart remained in close touch with the armoured force. He continued to preach his idea of deep strategic penetration when technical advancement (especially in radio communication), the beginning of rearmament, and the creation of the first permanent armoured formations made this idea realizable. Through his close association with Hobart he contributed considerably to the shaping of the latter's sweeping manoeuvres in 1934–37, which Liddell Hart also closely analysed and propagated from the pages of *The Daily Telegraph* and *The Times*. Furthermore, by 1935–37 Liddell Hart had realized that in the expected European theatres of operations the increasing density of forces and the lack of open flanks would make rapid breakthroughs of fronts, quick exploitation for ever-deeper penetrations, and the creation of 'inner flanks' the most promising method of operation for armoured forces. This was the method the Germans were to employ in 1939–41.

Finally, from the late 1920s Fuller began to realize that the offensive force of the tank would be met in a constant struggle for supremacy by its defensive capability and by anti-tank devices. Picking up these ideas, Liddell Hart claimed during the second half of the 1930s that against well-equipped mobile defence in depth, swift armour breakthroughs were becoming increasingly unlikely to succeed. Too eager to devise a defensive posture for the Western Allies, he was surprised and disgraced by France 1940. However, later in the war the 'Blitzkrieg' was blunted by the same means and techniques that Fuller, Liddell Hart (and the Soviet pioneers of 'Deep Battle') had foreseen in the 1930s.

British armour development during the interwar period worked as an inspiration and spur for action for all the great powers' armies. From the outset the German army was the most susceptible to the influence of the new British school. The mystique of German military excellence and the brilliant performance of the Panzer forces in the early phase of the Second World War make it difficult to comprehend how respectfully and even humbly the Reichswehr studied the developments in the armies of the victorious western powers. Objectively, Germany was a continental power with open borders and many potential enemies, and thus her army had long put the premium on swift operations aiming at a quick decision. The lessons of the First World War seemed to reinforce this traditional emphasis. Against a superior great power coalition which would be created against her, it was universally believed that Germany had to harness all her resources for war, but also fight unconventionally and win quickly, if she were to win at all. Even though there was never before the Second World War a German official or unofficial doctrine of 'Blitzkrieg', devised by either Hitler or the military, these considerations were paramount in everybody's minds.

Considering the restrictions within which it was operating, the Reichswehr in the early 1920s at least in theory gave ample attention to tanks and mechanized vehicles. Yet a crucial turning-point was reached when the far-reaching potential of the British Vickers Medium Tank for a revival of the war of movement, as revealed in the British manoeuvres, was noted in Germany from 1924 on. Simultaneously, the new British theories of future mechanized warfare came to the attention of the Reichswehr, first through Liddell Hart's articles and *Paris*, and slightly later but with great exposure, from Fuller's own works. In a remarkably short time, between 1924 and 1927, the two British exponents of armoured warfare became household names in German military circles. As the Reichswehr depended almost exclusively on open printed sources for information on the subject, these two prolific writers virtually monopolized the scene in Germany, though the 'practical men' in the Royal Armoured Corps were also known from their articles. Martel in particular won recognition when his book *In the Wake of the Tank* appeared in 1931 and was translated into German. Following the British manoeuvres (and the withdrawal of the Inter-Allied Control Commission from Germany in 1927) the Reichswehr began to take its first steps towards the creation of independent mechanized units and formations and officially endorsed the concept of strategic (*operativ*) employment of armour. Experimental tank models, ordered in the second half of the 1920, were tried out in the Soviet Union in the late 1920s and early 1930s. Leading the new trend in the higher levels of the Reichswehr and clandestine general staff were Generals Blomberg and Heye and the then Colonel Fritsch, especially the first named, but a wider group of junior and middle-rank officers was active below them. In this group Guderian was, until the early 1930s, only one and far from a leading member.

From 1932 onward, and especially after Hitler's rise to power, the German army was moving towards rearmament. The creation of tank units and the acquisition of a large number of tanks were an integral part of this process. Yet for what role exactly these tanks were to be designed, organized, and employed was a question about which opinions diverged. Under the impression of the latest British manoeuvres with the experimental mobile division in 1934, Beck, the chief of the general staff, was progressively giving way to the pressure from the Command of the Panzer Troops, in which Guderian was now the chief of staff and the driving force. Beck agreed to the creation of Panzer divisions, whose mission was independent strategic (*operativ*) penetrations. These divisions were basically built on the British model of 1934, and their operational doctrine was similarly adopted from the British school. Yet, looking to developments in all the great powers' armies, themselves beginning to undergo rearmament, Beck also wanted motorized infantry divisions, light mechanized divisions, and tanks for infantry close support. The ensuing technical argument was of crucial historical significance, for Beck planned that only the smaller part of German tanks would be incorporated in armoured divisions. He was thus in permanent strife with Guderian. As always, 'objective conditions' *as well as* ideas, personalities, and individual choices of people in positions of power were decisive in shaping the course of history.

Throughout the mid-1930s the Germans were continuing to keep track of Hobart's manoeuvres with the 1st Tank Brigade, in which deep strategic sweeps were repeatedly tried out. Reports from the military attaché in London were eagerly followed in the general staff, In.6, and the Command of the Panzer Troops, and so were also Liddell Hart's reports in *The Times* and in *When Britain Goes to War*. In late summer 1937 the Panzer division's potential was impressively demonstrated in the great Wehrmacht manoeuvres. From then on the Panzer arm left the British armoured forces definitely behind, though respect for the British armour pioneers remained very high. Even during the war, articles by Liddell Hart and Fuller were monitored by German intelligence and regularly and prominently printed in German journals. On one recorded occasion Rommel cited such an article by Liddell Hart, and Guderian read out another in a conference with Hitler and senior German generals in order to drive home ideas he shared with the author. The British theorists and the British seminal concept of armoured warfare had always been, and continued to be, a closely studied authority for the creators of the Panzer arm.

The historiographical conclusions of all this are not difficult to see. Leaving behind the conjectures and extrapolations from Liddell Hart's disputed papers and turning to the interwar German records themselves, the results produced may appear either exciting or dull. The traditional view of a decisive British influence on the formation of the Panzer arm returns with a vengeance, with some important modifications but on the whole greatly strengthened by often tantalizing documentation. True, Liddell Hart pressurized the German generals after the Second World War and then manipulated their evidence. But great as the German generals' debt to him at that time may have been, the idea that he could bring them to tell his desired story without the strongest foundation in reality should have been recognized on the face of it as incredible. Where they did not want to cooperate, they did not; and where they did, it was because what Liddell Hart wanted them to say was not far from what they knew to be true. From his point of view Liddell Hart was on the whole working to get the credit he knew was his due. Liddell Hart undoubtedly focused the whole story subjectively around himself, mainly at Fuller's expense. In addition, the paramount influence of the practical development of the pioneering British armoured force, in the context of which the influence of Fuller and Liddell Hart is to be understood, may not have been as clear to all those nourished on his version of events as it was to Liddell Hart himself. Still, the growth of the belief that that version was fundamentally false, for which Liddell Hart's own mischief is largely responsible, must be seen as a sobering lesson, if one is still needed, for the way historical myths may take root even in respect to relatively recent times and even in the scholarly community.

Notes

1 Liddell Hart's Theory of Armoured Warfare

1. Basil Henry Liddell Hart, *The Memoirs of Captain Liddell Hart* (London, 1965), i. 86; *idem*, 'Suggestions on the Future Development of the Combat Unit – the Tank as a Weapon of Infantry', *RUSI Journal* (Nov. 1919), 666–9; Jim Harper to LH, 6 Sept. 1919: 7/1919/6 (references are to LH's papers at King's College, London). LH's false pretence has been tacitly noted in Robin Higham, *The Military Intellectuals in Britain 1918–1939* (New Brunswick, NJ, 1966), 84–5; Harold Winton, *To Change an Army: General Sir John Burnett-Stuart and British Armoured Doctrine, 1927–1938* (Lawrence, Kansas, 1988), 38 n.67.
2. LH, 'H.G. Wells as a False Prophet', unpublished article: 7/1918/25b. For Wells' forecasts of future society and future mechanized warfare see my *Fascist and Liberal Visions of War: Fuller, Liddell Hart, Douhet and Other Modernists* (Oxford, 1998), 8–12.
3. LH to Fuller, 23 April 1948, in 1/302, taking sentences out of their original context and intent; misleading in the same manner is LH, *Memoirs*, i. 89–90.
4. Fuller to LH, 25 Aug. 1920, 1/302.
5. For Fuller's vision of future mechanized war see 'J.F.C. Fuller: Positivism, Evolution, Fascism, and Future Warfare', in my *Fascist and Liberal Visions of War*, 13–42.
6. LH to Fuller, 16 and 31 Jan. 1922 (citation from the later date); Fuller to LH, 19 Jan. 1922, 1/302.
7. LH, 'Are Infantry Doomed?', *The National Review* (May 1922), 455–63; *idem*, 'Infantry – "The New Model"', *ibid*. (July 1922), 712–22; *idem*, 'The Future Development of Infantry', *ibid*. (Oct. 1922), 286–94.
8. Fuller to LH, 18 Dec. 1922, 1/302; LH, *Memoirs*, i. 91–2.
9. LH, 'The Next Great War', *The Royal Engineers Journal* (March 1924), 90–107.
10. LH, 'The Development of the "New Model" Army, Suggestions on a Progressive, but Gradual Mechanization', *The Army Quarterly* (Oct. 1924), 37–50. Cf. Fuller, 'Gold Medal (Military) Prize Essay for 1919: "The Application of Recent Developments in Mechanics and Other Scientific Knowledge to Preparation and Training for Future War on Land"', *RUSI Journal*, 65 (1920), 239–74.
11. Only a couple of historians have noted this briefly. As Brian Holden Reid, *J.F.C. Fuller: Military Thinker* (London, 1987), 225, has written: 'the similarity in the approach, content and style of Fuller's *The Reformation of War* and Liddell Hart's *Paris* is striking though rarely remarked upon.'; also Michael Carver, *The Apostles of Mobility* (London, 1979), 43–4.
12. LH, *Paris, or the Future of War* (London, 1925), 41–89; the reference to 'Plan 1919' (pp. 82–3) is the only direct citation from Fuller.
13. See e.g. LH's briefing of John Wheldon, *Machine Age Armies* (London, 1968), 33–8.

14 See more fully in my *Fascist and Liberal Visions of War*, 143–150 and *passim*.
15 LH, *Memoirs*, i. 90–1.
16 But see the significant time distinction *ibid*. i. 270.
17 John Mearsheimer, *Liddell Hart and the Weight of History* (London, 1988), 33–46.
18 Jay Luvaas, *The Education of an Army: British Military Thought, 1815–1940* (London, 1965), 405.
19 This is fast becoming the accepted view; cf. J.P. Harris, 'British Armour 1918–40: Doctrine and Development', in his and F.H. Toase (eds), *Armoured Warfare* (London, 1990), 29, claiming that LH had no theory of armoured warfare other than what he wrote in *Paris*; also his *Men, Ideas and Tanks: British Military Thought and Armoured Forces, 1903–1939* (Manchester, 1995).
20 This historiographical 'black hole' is evident in LH's works consulted in Luvaas, *loc. cit.* For the works referred to by Mearsheimer see his *LH*, 35 n. He mentions, but fails to cite, a 'handful' of *Daily Telegraph* columns, primarily relying on Liddell Hart's later private list which incorporated extracts from those columns: 'Suggestions and Forecasts: Salient Points from Captain Liddell Hart's Articles in *The Daily Telegraph*, 1925–1934', 13/3; this list could have in fact led to much of the relevant material, had it been used properly.
21 LH, *The Tanks* (London, 1959), i. 241–54; *idem, Memoirs*, i. 107–36; Winton, *To Change an Army*, 72–105.
22 LH, *The Daily Telegraph*, 31 Aug. 1927.
23 LH, *The Daily Telegraph*, 10 Sept. 1927; *idem, The Tanks*, i. 251–2; *idem, Memoirs*, i. 129.
24 The quotation is from LH, 'Medieval Cavalry and Modern Tanks', *English Review* (July 1925), 91; also published in the *Atlantic Monthly* (Sept. 1925) and in *The Royal Tank Corps Journal* (Oct. 1925). See also, less directly but still clear enough: 'Two Great Captains: Jenghiz Khan and Subutai', *Blackwood's Magazine* (May 1924), 644–59; incorporated in LH, *Great Captains Unveiled* (London, 1927), 1–34.
25 See e.g. *The Daily Telegraph*, 9 Sept. 1927, 23 Aug. 1928, 31 Aug. 1934; 'The New British Doctrine of Mechanized War', *The English Review* (Dec. 1929), 700.
26 *The Daily Telegraph*, 29 Aug., 4 and 22 Sept. 1928.
27 *Ibid.* 25 Aug. 1928.
28 *Ibid.*; reproduced in LH, *Thoughts on War* (London, 1944), 53–4.
29 *The Daily Telegraph*, 26 Sept. and 28 Nov. 1928; the former reprinted as 'Armoured Forces in 1928', *RUSI Journal* (Dec. 1928).
30 *Ibid.* quotation from p. 723.
31 LH, 'The New British Doctrine of Mechanized War', 700; *idem*, 'The Future of Armament and Its Future Use', *Yale Review* (June 1930), 663; also published in *Royal Air Force Quarterly*, (Oct. 1930).
32 LH, 'The Army Exercises of 1930', *RUSI Journal* (Nov. 1930), 681–90; also in *The Daily Telegraph*, 25–6 Sept. 1930.
33 *The Daily Telegraph*, 16 Sept. 1932; LH, *When Britain Goes to War* (London, 1935), 276, 280.
34 *The Daily Telegraph*, 11 Nov. 1933.

35 LH, *Memoirs*, i. 238; *idem*, *The Tanks*, i. 306.
36 LH, *Memoirs*, i. 236–8; Hobart to Lindsay 10 Nov. 1933, 1/376; *The Tanks*, i. 305 and *seq*. Cf. Kenneth Macksey, *Armoured Crusader: a Biography of Major General Sir Percy Hobart* (London, 1967), 117–18.
37 See Hobart's echoing of LH's ideas, esp. in his letter of 7 Oct. 1934, and his reference to LH's enormous influence on the 1934–37 manoeuvres, 19 Jan. 1946: 1/376. Cf. Macksey, *Armoured Crusader*, 117–18, 136.
38 LH, *The Tanks*, i. 307–8. Again cf. Hobart to LH, 7 Oct. 1934, 1/376.
39 *The Daily Telegraph*, 28 Aug. 1934; see also *ibid*. 14 Aug. 1928; *The New York Times Magazine*, 2 Dec. 1934; rep. in *The Sunday Chronicle*, 27 Jan. 1935.
40 LH, *The Tanks*, i. 339; *Memoirs*, i. 264.
41 *The Times*, 23, 24 and 27 Aug. 1935; the passage of 24 Aug. was reproduced in LH, *Thoughts on War*, 55.
42 Mearsheimer, *LH*, 43.
43 Robert Larson, *The British Army and the Theory of Armoured Warfare 1918–1940* (Newark, Delaware, 1984), 163–7, 170; Mearsheimer was apparently unfamiliar with this book. Hobart's manoeuvres of August 1934 are not covered by Winton's excellent *To Change an Army*, because the hero of his book, General Burnett-Stuart, was not involved in them, having just returned from a three-year tenure as commander-in-chief in Egypt; but see *ibid*. 123. Hobart's historical manoeuvres of 1934–37 are curiously not even mentioned by J. Paul Harris, 'Sir Percy Hobart', in Brian Bond (ed.), *Fallen Stars, Eleven Studies of Twentieth Century Military Disasters* (London, 1991), 86–106.
44 This also has the effect of making *The Tanks* a far more balanced book than *Memoirs*.
45 Cf. LH's views in 1933, *When Britain Goes to War*, 278–9.
46 *The Times*, 18 Sept. 1935.
47 *Ibid*. 10 Sept. 1937; reproduced in LH, *The Defence of Britain* (London, 1939), 376–8, and *Memoirs*, ii. 25–6.
48 *The Times*, 25 Oct. 1937. More on mechanized long-range strategic penetration can be found *ibid*. 4 May 1936 and 1 Oct. 1937.
49 E.g. LH, *Defence of the West* (London, 1950), 269.
50 11/1932/49. The point about the 'tactical base' had already been strongly alluded to in LH, *Great Captains Unveiled* (London, 1927), 32. In a later edition of *Lectures of FSR III* Fuller acknowledged his omission in respect to close ground–air cooperation: *Armoured Warfare* (London, 1943), Preface, 28–9, 106–7; he had always believed that the ground-attack aircraft and the tank were the weapons of the future, but not necessarily working in close cooperation; for LH's advocacy of such cooperation see e.g. *The Daily Telegraph*, 19 June 1926; *The Defence of Britain*, 299.
51 This crucial point has been relegated to an obscure note: Mearsheimer, *LH*, 208 n.97.
52 Letter exchange in Feb. 1964, in 1/302. See also A.J. Trythal, *'Boney' Fuller: the Intellectual General* (London, 1977), 60–4, 71, 73.
53 Reid, *Fuller*, 151.
54 See e.g. LH, 'Contrasts of 1931, Mobility or Stagnation', *Army Quarterly* (Jan. 1932), 235ff, rep. in *When Britain Goes to War*, 213–15, also 261–2; *The Times*, 27 Aug. 1935 and 1 Sept. 1937; LH, *The Tanks*, i. 327, 348. Cf.

Victor Germains's scathing criticism, *The 'Mechanization' of War* (London, 1927), 229.
55 Macksey, *The Tank Pioneers* (London, 1981), 83; Mearsheimer, *LH*, 39; LH in *The Daily Telegraph*, 28 Aug. 1925; rep. in *The Remaking of Modern Armies* (London, 1927), Ch. 5; Broad to LH, 29 June 1932, in 1/108; *When Britain Goes to War*, 265; and, somewhat misleadingly, in *Memoirs*, i. 77–8.
56 13 July 1925, 5/12/1 (apparently missing); cited in LH, *The Tanks*, i. 231.
57 Hobart to Lindsay, 10 July 1925, this and the whole of the following correspondence are in 15/12/13; cited *ibid*. 231–2.
58 Lindsay to Hobart, 21 Aug. 1925, *ibid*. 232–3. For LH's influence cf. his *Defence of the West*, 269, published when Lindsay was still alive.
59 Hobart to Lindsay, 10 July 1925, Lindsay to Hobart, 21 Aug. 1925, *The Tanks*, i. 231–2; on the efforts in the late 1920s and early 1930s to develop radio communication for the armoured units see pp. 267, 325–6.
60 Macksey, *The Tank Pioneers*, 79–88, makes this point very well.
61 *The Tanks*, i. 286–7, 290–3; *Memoirs*, i. 179–81.
62 The booklet can be found in LH's Special Bookcase. Cf. Harris, 'British Armour', in his and Toase, *Armoured Warfare*, 38–9.
63 LH, *Memoirs*, i. 160.
64 Mearsheimer, *LH*, 109–16, is generally accurate about the development of LH's ideas on the superiority of defence.
65 The problem of defining certain weapon systems as either defensive or offensive is not our concern here. Winston Churchill anticipated the arguments against that distinction when he said in Parliament, after the idea had become official British policy, that it was a 'silly expedient', for the character of weapons is determined by the way they are used and by the politics they serve rather than by their inherent qualities. Liddell Hart made the opposite case no less ably in his response: 'Would the Scrapping of Heavy Guns and Tanks Cripple the Aggressor's Power?', *The Daily Telegraph*, 1 Feb. 1932; also 'Aggression and the Problem of Weapons', *The English Review*, July 1932, 71–8 (a reply to Fuller), quotation from 71–2; the story is summarized in *Memoirs*, i. 183–93, 207–10, quotation from 186; LH, *Europe in Arms* (London, 1937), 143–4.
66 See extensively in my treatment of LH in *Fascist and Liberal Visions of War*, passim.
67 See e.g. *Europe in Arms*, 339–56; *The Defence of Britain*, 118–20.
68 *Ibid*; *The Spectator*, 17 Nov. 1933, 738–40; *The New York Times Magazine*, 2 Dec. 1934, 3, 18; *The Times*, 17 Aug., 19 Sept., 27 Nov. 1935, 21 Aug. 1936.
69 Fuller, 'One Hundred Problems of Mechanization', Part Two, *The Army Quarterly*, 19 (1929), 256–8. For a balanced assessment from the second half of the 1930s see Fuller, 'The Problem of Tank and Anti-Tank Weapons', *The Fighting Forces*, 14 (1937), 42–5.
70 *The Times*, 26 Nov. 1935, reprinted in *Europe in Arms*, 83; also see *The Times*, 23 March 1936.
71 LH, *The Times*, 21 May 1937; 'Military and Strategic Advantages of Collective Security in Europe', *New Commonwealth Quarterly* (Sept. 1938), 144, reprinted in Europe in Arms, 54; also see, for the same ideas, *The Times*, 30 Oct., 2 Nov. 1936, reprinted in *Europe in Arms*, 118; *ibid*, 125–9,

138–9; *The Defence of Britain*, 120–1. None of these passages was marked by LH for inclusion in the list of his successful forecasts (13/3), which he carefully compiled for the writing of his *Memoirs*. Cf. Germains, *The 'Mechanization' of War*, 47–54, 74–89.

72 For the counter-argument that armour still enjoyed the advantages of initiative and concentration, see both Tukhachevsky, 'The Red Army New (1936) Field Service Regulations', *Red Star*, 6 May 1937, printed in Richard Simpkin, *Deep Battle: the Brainchild of Marshal Tukhachevski* (London, 1987), 161–2; Heinz Guderian, *Achtung Panzer! The Development of Armoured Forces, Their Tactics and Operational Potential* (London, 1992; German original 1937), 154–8, 169.

73 LH, 'Spain – Attack or Defence', *The Times*, 3 April 1937; reprinted in *Europe in Arms*, 323–32.

74 LH, *The Times*, 21 May 1937.

75 Tukhachevsky, 'The Red Army Field Service Regulations', *Red Star*, 6 May 1937, in Simpkin, *Deep Battle*, 161–2. But see n. 72 above.

76 LH, 'The Futility of Aggression', *The Times*, 27 Oct. 1937; reprinted in *Europe in Arms*, 49–50.

77 See LH's paper on 'The Military Situation in Europe', given at the Staff College in Dec. 1937, printed in *The Defence of Britain*, esp. 55, 57, 59–60. For LH's strategic conception for the West vis-à-vis the Axis threat see my *Fascist and Liberal Visions of War*.

78 The connection is well pointed out by Mearsheimer, *LH*, 110–11, 115–16.

79 Meetings between Liddell Hart and Deverell, 12 Nov. 1936, 11/1936/99 (Haining attending); 29 June 1937, 11/1937/56; 18 Nov. 1937, 11/1937/94; cf. LH, *Memoirs*, i. 382–3, in which Haining's remark is not cited.

80 Talk with Hore-Belisha, 15 Oct. 1937, 11/HB 1937/56; not cited in LH's *Memoirs*. See also Wesley K. Wark, *The Ultimate Enemy: British Intelligence and Nazi Germany, 1933–1939* (London, 1985), 95–6.

81 LH's paramount role as the spirit behind H-B and as king-maker is amazingly revealed in his files: 11/1937/96 ff, 11/HB 1937–8; partly printed in *Memoirs*, ii. 62–74.

82 See in Mearsheimer, *LH*, 118.

83 See e.g. LH, 'The Defence of the Empire', *Fortnightly Review* (Jan. 1938), 27–9; *The Times*, 17 Sept. 1938; *The Defence of Britain*, 209–10.

84 LH, 'The Need for a New Technique', printed in *The Current of War*, (London, 1941) 152; Barrington-Ward to LH, 27 Oct. 1939, 3/109, rejecting it for publication in *The Times* on the grounds that according to his sources the Allies had no intention of attacking in the west.

85 LH, 'Gamelin', *Life Magazine*, 20 Feb. 1939, 56–63; *Sunday Express*, 29 Oct. 1939 and 18 Feb. 1940; *The Current of War*, 205, 209; Mearsheimer, *LH*, 124. LH's unfavourable testimony regarding Gamelin in *Memoirs*, ii. 18, tilts the original record, and has misled Martin Alexander, *The Republic in Danger: General Maurice Gamelin and the Politics of French Defence, 1933–1940* (Cambridge, 1992), 274; but for the generally warm reception of Gamelin during his visits to Britain in the years preceding the war and for his objection to any offensive ventures during the Polish campaign and the Phoney War, see respectively Alexander, 'Maurice Gamelin', in Bond (ed.), *Fallen Stars*, 108, 119; idem, *Gamelin*, 279ff. For Ironside's opposition

to an encounter battle in Belgium see *The Ironside Diaries, 1937–1940* (London, 1962), 108. Gamelin was very highly regarded by the Germans, e.g. by Beck and Rundstedt who both met him in 1936–37: Reynolds, *Treason was no Crime: Ludwig Beck, Chief of the German General Staff* (London 1976), 111–15; Earl F. Ziemke, 'Rundstedt', in Correlli Barnett (ed.), *Hitler's Generals* (London, 1989), 188.

86 Norman Gibbs, *Grand Strategy*, i (London, 1976), 637.
87 For LH's painstaking efforts to save face, responding cleverly but all too often misleadingly to every one of the many letters to the press which especially during the early war years touched upon the source of his disgrace, see Section 6 of his papers; a selection can be found in Mearsheimer, *LH*, 152–4.
88 For LH's 'apologia' see mainly his *Dynamic Defence* (London, 1940), 12–41, 57–64; *The Current of War* (London, 1941), 15–125, 193–4, 208–9, 214, 316, 320–2, 328–9, 337–8; both books reprint large extracts from his early writings on the subject of armoured warfare; *The Revolution in Warfare* (London, 1946), 15–16, 28–9; *Defence of the West*, 3–11; *Memoirs*, ii. 28, 242–4, 280–1.
89 LH, *Europe in Arms*, 116–40; *The Times*, 25 Oct. 1937; also 2 Nov. 1936.
90 *Europe in Arms*, 122–3, 228; in the British army this policy was carried out by Hugh Elles and Q. Martel in their tenures, respectively, at the Master-General of the Ordnance Department and the Directorate of Mechanization.
91 See LH, *The Times*, 23 Dec. 1935, 19 July 1938; *Fortnightly Review* (Jan. 1938), 26–7; *Life Magazine*, 20 Feb. 1939, p. 62; *Europe in Arms*, 43–4, 49–51. That he was now biased for the French is rightly pointed out by Mearsheimer, *LH*, 122–3.
92 In March 1941, while correctly assessing the number of German mobile divisions, Allied intelligence estimated the German tank force at 5800–7500, two to three times the actual number: F.H. Hinsley, *British Intelligence in the Second World War*, i (London, 1979), 134. But see Guderian to LH, 14 Dec. 1948: 9/24/62.
93 See e.g. LH, *The Times*, 21 May 1937. Again this had been Fuller's view at least since the late 1920s.
94 See e.g. *Europe in Arms*, 27–8, 48; *The Defence of Britain*, 101. For the British picture of German armour see excellently in Wark, *British Intelligence*, 93–101, who stresses, however, how assessment was affected by the disputes within both the German and British high commands regarding the role of armour. For the French, see Robert Young, 'French Military Intelligence and Nazi Germany, 1938–1939', in Ernest R. May (ed.), *Knowing One's Enemies: Intelligence Assessment before the Two World Wars* (Princeton, 1984), 288–9.
95 Gort's comments on LH's 'Defence or Attack', 6 Nov. 1937, 11/1937/73; Bond, *LH*, 118; Mearsheimer, *LH*, 81.
96 Conversation with Deverell, 29 June 1937, 11/1937/56; *The Ironside Diaries*, 38.
97 See p. 12 above.
98 LH, 'The Next Big War', *The Listener*, 15 March 1936.
99 LH, *Atlantic Monthly* (Dec. 1936), 693; similar ideas in 'Future Warfare',

English Review (May 1937), 529–43; and 'The Defence of the Empire', *Fortnightly Review* (Jan. 1938), 19–30.
100 LH, *The Times*, 25 Oct. 1937; this extract is reprinted in *The Defence of Britain*, 105. None of the above passages is cited by Mearsheimer. After conceding that, defensively employed, the tank 'can thwart a blitzkrieg', he writes that in LH's 'pieces on the strength of the defense, especially those written in the late 1930s, he failed to discuss the significant offensive potential of the tank when a defender does not understand how to employ tanks on the battlefield (i.e., he fails to emphasize that a blitzkrieg was possible under certain circumstances)': Mearsheimer, LH, 113–14.
101 He was of course not alone in developing this idea. The Soviets developed it by far the most systematically in their 1936 Field Service Regulations, and it was also well recognized by the Germans. See in Simpkin, *Deep Battle*, 47–8, 172–3; Ritter von Leeb, *Defence* (Harisburg, Pa., 1943; original in *Militärwissenschaftliche Rundschau*, 1936–1937), 109–110.
102 For all the above see LH, *The Times*, 30 Oct. 1936; 'The Defence of the Empire', *Fortnightly Review* (Jan. 1938), 24–9; *Europe in Arms*, 27–8, 47–8; *The Defence of Britain*, 55, 60, 104–5, 210, 307, 376–81.
103 See Henry Dutailly, *Les Problèmes de l'armée de terre française (1935–1939)* (Paris, 1980), 141–59, 314–37; Alexander, *Gamelin and the Politics of French Defence*, 201–2; Robert A. Doughty, *The Seeds of Disaster: the Development of French Army Doctrine 1919–1939* (Hamden, CT, 1985), 161–77. LH was well informed about these developments at the time: *Europe in Arms*, 43–4.
104 For Fuller see his 'Tanks Won't Do Much', *The War Weekly*, 19 Nov. 1939, 11/1939/146; for LH see e.g. *The Defence of Britain*, 55–60, and 11 May 1940, reprinted in *The Current of War*, 301.
105 Quoted by John Mearsheimer, *Conventional Deterrence* (Ithaca and London, 1983), 102, 108.
106 The best analysis of the Allies' strategic considerations is Jeffery A. Gunsburg, *Divided and Conquered: the French High Command and the Defeat of the West, 1940* (London, 1979).
107 Winston Churchill, *The Second World War* (London, 1948–55), ii. 46–7.
108 See initially, LH, *The Defence of Britain*, 216–19; then, *Dynamic Defence*, 18, *The Current of War*, 209, 316, 337; finally, 'Could the 1940 Collapse in the West Have Been Averted?', *Sunday Pictorial*, 28 Sept. 1947; reproduced in *The Defence of the West*, 3–19; and as an Introduction to Goutard, *1940 – the Battle of France* (London 1958).
109 Although recent research has done much to show the logic behind the Allies' plans, it reaffirms that they (and Gamelin in particular) totally blundered in respect to the Ardennes: Robert J. Young, *In Command of France: French Foreign Policy and Military Planning 1933–1940* (Cambridge Mass., 1978), 169; Umbreit's contribution to Militärgschichtles Forschungsamt (MF) (ed.), *Germany in the Second World War*, ii. 271; Claude Paillat, *Le Désastre de 1940*, i (Paris, 1983), 191–6; Alexander, *Gamelin*, 199–200.
110 LH, *The Decisive Wars of History* (London, 1929), 225; similarly see his *The Real War* (London, 1930), 461; *Foch* (London, 1931), 383; *A History of the World War* (London, 1934), 577.
111 15 May 1936: 11/1936/64; again cited by Bond, *LH*, 101, 232–3, but not by Mearsheimer, *LH*, 182–3, although he was familiar with LH's reference list

composed after the war to make his case regarding the Ardennes: 14 Dec. 1948; 11/1948/28.
112 LH, *The Defence of Britain*, 217–19.
113 Reprinted in *The Current of War*, 299–300, 304, 309–10, 315–17, 338–44.
114 On the whole operation see Robert A. Doughty, *The Breaking Point: Sedan and the Fall of France, 1940* (Hamden, CT, 1990). For the Belgian and French reading of German intentions in this respect see Brian Bond, *France and Belgium, 1939–1940* (London, 1975), 60–1, 64–5, 76–7, 78–80; Hinsley, *British Intelligence*, i. 129–36; Paillat, *1940*, ii (Paris, 1984), 299–354; Doughty, *op. cit.*, 73–7. For Ironside's prediction regarding the Ardennes see *The Ironside Diaries*, 120–1, 125, also pointing out Gamelin's intransigence.
115 LH, *Memoirs*, ii. 243. See also Mearsheimer, *LH*, esp. 179–81, 216–17.
116 LH, *Dynamic Defence*, 26, 52–4; also see his opinions *at the time* regarding the Soviet Union's prospects of defence in June 1941 and regarding the Western Desert, where he was interestedly following Rommel's use of anti-tank guns and defensive tactics within an offensive strategy (much of his later interest in Rommel derived from the latter's ideas on defence in Normandy and the Eastern Front, *The Rommel Papers* (London, 1953), 451–60): *This Expanding War*, (London 1942) 72–3, 138–40; *The Revolution in Warfare*, 15–23, 29; *Memoirs*, ii. 281.
117 11/1932/49.
118 Macksey, *Armoured Crusader*, 74–5.
119 Regarding infantry see Reid, *Fuller*, 161.
120 LH to Fuller, 23 Apr. and 5 May 1948, 1/302.
121 See e.g. Fuller's RUSI Gold Medal essay, and 'Tanks in Future Warfare', *The Nineteenth Century and After* (July 1921); reprinted in *On Future Warfare* (London, 1928), 148.
122 Fuller, 'Problems of Mechanized Warfare', *The Army Quarterly* (Jan. 1922), incorporated in *The Reformation of War*, 161–4, and reprinted in *On Future Warfare*, 248–51; 'The Ideal Army of the Artillery Circle', *The Journal of the Royal Artillery*, (Oct. 1926), and 'Tactics and Mechanization', *The Fighting Forces* (Apr. 1927), reprinted in *On Future Warfare*, 368–70, 233–7 respectively; *Armoured Warfare*, 19–21, 95; *Towards Armageddon* (London, 1937), 140–1. Reid's assessment in *Fuller*, 161–3, is similar to mine, but does not make it clear that Fuller assigned his light infantry to 'infantry areas' only.
123 LH, 'Are Infantry Doomed?', *The National Review* (1922), 457–8; see also the other infantry articles mentioned in n. 7 above; 'The Next Great War', *The Royal Engineers Journal* (1924), 107; 'New Model Army', *The Army Quarterly* (1924), 44–5; *Paris*, 88.
124 *Paris*, 88.
125 LH, *The Remaking of Modern Armies*, 9, 15; *idem*, 'The New British Doctrine of Mechanized War', *The English Review* (Dec. 1929), 699; *idem*, *When Britain Goes to War*, 261.
126 See LH, *The Tanks*, i. 247–8; *Memoirs*, i. 124, 161–2; Winton, *To Change an Army*, 94. LH's comments at the time were reprinted in *When Britain Goes to War*, 172.
127 *The Tanks*, i. 269–70, 296; *Memoirs*, i. 161–2; *To Change an Army*, 82.
128 Lindsay, 'The Organization and Employment of a Mechanized Force', 25 April 1924, and other memos from the same year in 15/12/6; *The Tanks*, i.

208, 247–8, 329; Lindsay to Hobart, 17 Nov. 1933, Bridgeman papers, LHCMA, file 5, esp. the letter attached to 5/3; Winton, *To Change an Army*, 178; Harris, 'British Armour', 34.
129 Hobart to Lindsay, 10 Nov. 1933, attached to 'Use of Armoured and Mechanized Forces in the Early Stages of a European War', 1/376; Lindsay to Hobart, 17 Nov. 1933, the whole correspondence between the two is in 15/12/8; *The Tanks*, i. 329; *To Change an Army*, 177–8; Macksey, *The Tank Pioneers*, 128–32.
130 *The Tanks*, i. 230–1, 258–9, 324–5; Winton, *To Change an Army*, 231–2; Brian Bond, *British Military Policy between the Two World Wars* (Oxford, 1980), 144–5, 165–6.
131 A conversation with Hobart, 13 Nov. 1936, 11/1936/94; Hobart to LH, 6 Dec. 1936, 1/376; a conversation with Deverell, 18 Nov. 1937, 11/1937/94; *Memoirs*, i. 383; memorandum to Hore-Belisha, *Memoirs*, ii. 46–7, also 58–9; Macksey, *Armoured Crusader*, 144–6; Winton, *To Change an Army*, 193–5, 231.
132 LH, 'The Army in 1935 – Signs of Recovery', *English Review* (Feb. 1935), 152; reprinted in *When Britain Goes to War*, 261, also 263–6.
133 LH, *The Tanks*, i. 329; *Memoirs*, i. 125.
134 Macksey, *Armoured Crusader*, 138–40; also Hobart to LH, 23 Nov. 1937, 1/376.
135 31 Jan. 1938, 11/HB 1938/27; *The Defence of Britain*, 298–300; *Memoirs*, ii. 57.
136 R.M. Ogorkiewicz, *Armoured Forces* (London, 1970), 59.
137 *Ibid*. 60.
138 *Ibid*. 60–1, 88–93; S.D. Badsey, 'The American Experience of Armour 1919–1953', in Harris and Toase (eds), *Armoured Warfare*, 130–42.
139 LH, 'When Are We Going to Adjust Ourselves to Mechanized Warfare?', memorandum of 11 June 1941, printed in LH, *This Expanding War*, 222–3; note of Jan. 1942, printed *ibid*. 268.
140 See in 11/1942i.
141 For both sides of the controversy see the somewhat partisan accounts in Giffard le Q. Martel, *An Outspoken Soldier* (London, 1949), 67, 124–5, 175, 178, 183–4, 188; Macksey, *Armoured Crusader*, 185–227, *The Tank Pioneers*, 172–6.
142 Martel to LH, 1 Apr. 1943, 1/492. Martel had his own cross to carry; in the late 1930s he shared responsibility for the decision to develop the two different types designated 'infantry' and 'cruiser' tanks, a decision which plagued the British army throughout the war: Martel, *An Outspoken Soldier*, 124–35, 162–74, 205–210, 273, 285, 322–4.
143 LH, 23 Sept. 1942, 11/1942/79; 21 Dec. 1942, 11/1942/106, published in *The Daily Mail*, 31 Dec. 1942; LH to Martel, 8 Apr. 1943, 1/492.
144 LH, 26 Oct. 1943, 11/1943/67; 28 Oct. 1944, 11/1944/62, citing Brooke's statement that the power of the tank was on the wane (cf. Martel, *An Unspoken Soldier*, 276–7); *Defence of the West*, 267, 280–9; *Deterrent or Defence* (London, 1960), 185–200. Fuller, too, continued to advocate similar ideas during the war; see e.g. 6 and 16 April 1943, in his *Watchwords* (London, 1944), 46–50.
145 LH to Martel, 24 Jan. 1946, 22 Dec. 1951: 1/492; see also his summary of his position: 11/1948/36.

146 Heinz Guderian, *Panzer Leader*, (London, 1952), 294–5; he probably referred to LH's article of 31 Dec. 1942, mentioned in n. 143 above; the authenticity of Guderian's evidence is beyond question, for he had not been advised on this point by LH, who was himself surprised and delighted to read it in the Guderian memoirs: LH to Broad, 28 Dec. 1951, 1/108. Generally on their objection to the decrease see also Thoma's evidence, 9/24/144; Guderian to LH, 14 Dec. 1948 and 24 Jan, 1949, 9/24/62.

2 British Influence and the Evolution of the Panzer Arm

1 Kenneth Macksey in 'Liddell Hart: the Captain Who Taught Generals', *The Listener*, 28 Dec. 1972, 895; *idem, Guderian: Panzer General* (London, 1975), 40–1; *idem, The Tank Pioneers*, 118, 216; elaborated and expanded by Mearsheimer, *LH*, 160–7, 184–201.
2 See esp. in 9/24; Bond, *LH*, 180–8, 227–8. LH fiercely rejected any evidence of the German generals' ties with Nazism and involvement in the persecution of the Jews, which was presented to him by his friend, the great (Jewish) historian Louis Namier: the latter's comments on *The Other Side of the Hill* and letter exchange of 4 and 11 April 1951, in 1/539.
3 Manstein files 9/24/71 and 9/24/124; Paget to LH 12 Apr. 1951, LH to Paget 1 May 1951, in 1/563; Reginald Paget, *Manstein: His Campaigns and His Trials* (London, 1951), 22; LH, *Memoirs*, ii. 203–4; Mearsheimer, *LH*, 188–9; Bond, *LH*, 232–3.
4 See 9/24/24, 9/24/50 and 1/776; *The Rommel Papers*, 203, 299, 520; Mearsheimer, *LH*, 191–201.
5 LH to Guderian, 12 Mar., 25 Feb., and 30 Apr. 1949; Guderian to LH, 2 Mar. and 30 July 1949: in 9/24/62.
6 6 May 1950, *ibid.*
7 LH to Guderian 25 Feb., 3 Mar., 9 and 28 Nov., 30 Dec. 1949.
8 Guderian, *Erinnerungen eines Soldaten* (Heidelberg, 1951), 15; LH to Guderian, 6 Apr. 1951; Guderian to Liddell Hart, 23 Apr. 1951: both in 9/24/62; *Panzer Leader* (London, 1952), 20 (significantly, perhaps, the last sentence and a half in the second paragraph was Guderian's own); Mearsheimer, *LH*, 164–5, 189–90.
9 Macksey, *Guderian*, 41; *idem, The Tank Pioneers*, 118; Mearsheimer, *LH*, 190–1.
10 Walter Nehring's useful *Die Geschichte der deutschen Panzerwaffe, 1916 bis 1945* (Berlin, 1969), was also written by a veteran of the Panzer arm and Guderian's subordinate.
11 James S. Corum, *The Roots of Blitzkrieg: Hans von Seeckt and German Military Reform* (Lawrence, Kans., 1992).
12 Heeresdienstvorschrift 487, *Führung und Gefecht der verbundenen Waffen*, (Berlin, 1923), esp. paragraphs 347, 362, 523–37, 551. Similarly see in the guidelines for an exercise prepared by the Inspekteur der Verkehrstruppen (In. 6[K]), 1 July 1924, in RH 39/115 (henceforth all German documentary references are to the Bundesarchiv/Militärarchiv (BA-MA), Freiburg im Breisgau). See also Corum, *Seeckt and German Military Reform*, 122–6.
13 Ernst Volckheim, *Die deutschen Kampfwagen im Weltkrieg* (Berlin, 1923); *idem, Der Kampfwagen in der heutigen Kriegsführung* (Berlin, 1924); *idem*, in

Militär-Wochenblatt, 25 July 1924, 718; 4 Aug. 1924, 119–22; 11 Oct. 1925, 465–8, and 18 April 1926, 1409–12. He was also the chief writer in six special supplementary issues to the journal, entitled *Der Kampfwagen* ('The Tank') and published monthly between Oct. 1924 and March 1925. An example of his work from August 1924 on tank instruction in the army can be found in RH 12–2/51. See also Corum, *Seeckt and German Military Reform*, 126–30.

14 Fritz Heigl, *Taschenbuch der Tanks* (Munich, 1926); expanded posthumous edns 1935, 1938; Heigl's contributions to *Militär-Wochenblatt* can be found in nearly every other issue. See also Corum, *Seeckt and German Military Reform*, 103.

15 See e.g. 14 Oct. 1924, in RH 39/115.

16 For the Heavy and Light Tractors see Walter Spielberger, *Die Motorisierung der deutschen Reichswehr 1920–1935* (Stuttgart, 1979), 281–350; Werner Oswald, *Kraftfahrzeuge und Panzer der Reichswehr, Wehrmacht und Bundeswehr* (Stuttgart, 1982), 340–6; Corum, *Seeckt and German Military Reform*, 112–18. On the cooperation with the Soviet Union see Manfred Zeidler, *Reichswehr und Rote Armee 1920–1933* (Munich, 1993), 188–98.

17 Volckheim, *Betrachtungen über Kampfwagen-Organisation und Verwendung. Zu einer Abhandlung des englischen Majors Sherbrooke* (Berlin, 1924), 1; idem, *Kampfwagen und Abwehr dagegen* (Berlin, 1925), 3, 9–10; both booklets reprinted from *Wissen und Wehr*; Heigl, *Taschenbuch der Tanks*, 78, 322–6.

18 *Militär-Wochenblatt*, 25 July 1924, 713–15; the article had already been briefly summarized when the relevant issue of the *Royal Engineers Journal* had been routinely reviewed: *ibid.* 5 May 1924, 578; for the second piece see *ibid.*, 11 Nov. 1924, 501.

19 'Gedanken über eine allmähliche Mechanisierung in der englischen Armee', *Militär-Wochenblatt*, 18 Dec. 1924, 649–51 (signed '21').

20 The *Militär-Wochenblatt* cuts of 5 May, 25 July, and 11 Nov. 1924, can be found in LH's archive: 7/1919/13. As early as 10 July 1925, long before anyone could anticipate the German future exploits, *The Daily Telegraph*'s announcement of LH's appointment as its military correspondent already mentioned among his achievements that 'The German Ministry of War translated for circulation to their army his scheme for the progressive mechanization of the army'; also see LH's record of achievements of 1930, 11/1930/41.

21 T3, 'Bemerkungen zu den englischen Manövern 1924', 1 Dec. 1924, esp. 4–5, 10–11, in RH 2/1603; other intelligence surveys of the British army are in the same file. See also Corum, *Seeckt and German Military Reform*, 132.

22 *Militär-Wochenblatt*, 11 Jan. 1925, 761–3 (signed '21').

23 *Militär-Wochenblatt*, 18 Sept. 1925, 382; for more on the Vickers Medium and on the manoeuvres see e.g. *ibid.*, 25 May 1925 (Heigl's), the speed of the tank is here put at 40–45 km/h; 4 Oct. 1925, 449; 25 Oct. 1925, 559; 4 Nov. 1925, 587; 4 Dec. 1925, 777, 784; 11 March 1926, 1215; 25 March 1926, 1287; 18 April 1926, 1414; *Kriegs- und militärorganisatorische Gedanken und Nachrichten aus dem Auslande*, 2 (1926), 5:13–14, summarizing the 1925 manoeuvres and stressing speed and their futuristic character.

24 *Militär-Wochenblatt*, 11 Dec. 1925, 771–2 (signed 'Mügge').
25 *Ibid.*, 18 July 1926, 87 (signed 'Mügge'); Fuller is cited in another article in the following page.
26 *Ibid.*, 11 Jan. 1926, 913–18 (signed '83'); the author expanded these themes in a three-part article: *ibid.*, 18 and 25 May, and 4 June 1926, 1559–62, 1591–5, 1628–30.
27 For *Paris* see *ibid.*, 4 Sept. 1925, 291; and the general staff's foreign literature journal *Kriegs- und Militärorganisationische Gedanken und Nachrichten aus dem Auslande*, 2 (1926), 8:23–6; see also e.g. his reports on Martel's one-man tank: *Militär-Wochenblatt*, 11 Sept. 1925 and 25 Jan. 1926, 472, 1007; *Kriegs-Gedanken aus dem Auslande* (1926), 16:17–8; LH's articles in *The Daily Telegraph* on a variety of issues are often cited in the journal.
28 *Militär-Wochenblatt*, 11 Oct. 1925, 469–72.
29 For some early references to Fuller, apart from those already cited, see *Militär-Wochenblatt*, 15 April 1924, 531; 11 Oct. 1925, 473. *Kriegs-Gedanken aus dem Auslande* (1926), 2:21–28, summarizes his ideas as described in *The Daily Telegraph* (by LH) where he was named only as 'a high-ranking British Officer'; also see *ibid.*, 6:10. On his official nomination, background, and views: *Militär-Wochenblatt*, 25 Feb. 1926, 1157.
30 *Militär-Wochenblatt*, 11 Aug. 1926, 201–2; *Kriegs-Gedanken aus dem Auslande*, 2 (1926), 9:5–31; 10:5–29; 11:14–31; both journals emphasized his official nomination and expressed the expectation that he would have decisive influence on the future development of the British army. An article by Fuller also opened the collection *Kampfwagen und Heeresmotorisierung* (Berlin, 1926): *Militär-Wochenblatt*, 11 Aug. 1926, 214.
31 Copies (n.d.) in RH 8/v. 1745 and 1939.
32 This is rightly pointed out by Corum, *Seeckt and German Military Reform*, esp. 103, 131, 142; however, influenced by the recent revelations regarding LH's manipulations of the evidence on the subject, Corum wholly underrated his influence on the Germans (141–2), as the following will attempt to show.
33 29 May 1926, in RH 2/2195; *Militär-Wochenblatt*, 4 Aug. 1926, 146; the German 'englisch' and 'England' will be regularly translated as 'British' and 'Britain'. See also Corum, *Seeckt and German Military Reform*, 132.
34 *Militär-Wochenblatt*, 25 Oct. 1926, 553–5. *The Daily Telegraph* (LH) is often cited, e.g. on tank fire on the move: *Militär-Wochenblatt*, 18 Nov. 1926 (signed '83'); the same in *Kriegs-Gedanken aus dem Auslande*, 2 (1926), 14:21–7.
35 10 Nov. 1926, in RH 39/115.
36 Cited by Michael Geyer, 'German Strategy in the Age of Machine Warfare, 1914–1945', in Peter Paret (ed.), *Makers of Modern Strategy* (Princeton, 1986), 559; Geyer, too, emphasizes the British influence in these years on the genesis of the Panzer arm.
37 *Militär-Wochenblatt*, 11 April 1927 (signed '99').
38 Announcements on the beginning of the manoeuvres appeared *ibid.*, 11 and 18 Sept. 1927, 353, 384; the report itself appeared on 11, 18, 25 Oct. and 4 Nov. 1927, 501–7, 540–3, 568–71, 607–8 (signed '96'); this time it was mainly based on *The Times* rather than on *The Daily Telegraph*. Interestingly, however, a translation of a *Sunday Times* article on the manoeuvres in *Kriegs Gedanken aus dem Auslande*, 4 (1928), 1:5–9, reads

(p.7; retranslated into English): 'As Captain Liddell Hart, perhaps our best military writer of the new school, writes in his new book' – a note in the German journal explains: *The Remaking of Modern Armies*.
39 In.6(K), 17 July 1928, in RH 39/115.
40 *Kriegs-Gedanken aus dem Auslande*, 4 (1928), 3:13–17; *Militär-Wochenblatt*, 25 Dec. 1927, 909–10. Also in the same issue, 893–4, on the Mechanized Force and criticism of Fuller in Britain as 'fanatic'; the report opens with the sentence: 'Britain is known as the leading country in the mechanization of the army.'
41 *Militär-Wochenblatt*, 25 Feb. 1928, 1219–20 (signed '96'); Guderian, *Panzer Leader*, 22; idem, *Achtung Panzer! The Development of Armoured Forces, Their Tactics and Operational Potential* (London, 1992; German original 1937), 167–8; idem, *Die Panzertruppen, und ihr Zusammenwirken mit den anderen Waffen* (Berlin, 1937), 15–16. See also Macksey, *Guderian*, 48–9.
42 *Militär-Wochenblatt*, 4 Oct. 1928, 495–6.
43 *Kriegs-Gedanken aus dem Auslande*, 3 (1927), 3:18–23; 4 (1928), 13:5–25, 14:5–28; also 15:5–10 for a review of the book in *The Fighting Forces*; *Militär-Wochenblatt*, 25 Jan. 1928, 1048–52.
44 *Kriegs-Gedanken aus dem Auslande*, 4 (1928), 23:6–9; 5 (1929), 17:4–13, 21:5–17; 6 (1930), 1:19–22, 2:12–19, 4:4–16, 8:5–19; 10:12–16; 16:5–12.
45 For Fuller, on top of what has already been cited, see e.g. *Militär-Wochenblatt*, 4 July 1927, 11; 11 Jan. 1928, 966–70; *Kriegs-Gedanken aus dem Ausland*, 3 (1927), 5:5–21; 4 (1928), 15:16–22; 5 (1929), 3:18–23; 13:7–13; 15:5–15; 6 (1930), 14:24–6. For LH see e.g. *Militär-Wochenblatt*, 11 April 1927, 1412; 4 Nov. 1928, 675; 18 Jan. 1929 (his visit to the Italian armour corps); *Kriegs-Gedanken aus dem Auslande*, 3 (1927), 6:20–1 (his critique of the French army); and numerous reports from *The Daily Telegraph* on the British army.
46 In addition to books already cited, see the reviews in *Militär-Wochenblatt* of Liddell Hart's *Scipio*, 25 Jan. 1927, 1027–8; *Great Captains Unveiled*, 4 Dec. 1927; *The Decisive Wars of History*, 18 Dec. 1929, 905–6; *Sherman*, 4 April 1930, 1466.
47 For criticisms of Fuller's *The Reformation of War* and *On Future Warfare* see e.g. *Militär-Wochenblatt*, 11 Sept. 1926, 321–3 (signed '12'); the consecutive 'Is Fuller Right?', ibid., 4 Dec. 1929, 808–9 (signed '21'), 4 Jan. 1930, 975–6 (signed '97'), 11 Jan. 1930, 1010–12 (signed '139'), all sensibly qualifying rather than rejecting. Germains's critical *The 'Mechanization' of War* was extensively summarized in three issues of *Kriegs-Gedanken aus dem Auslande*, 4 (1928), 16:5–28, 17:5–31, 18:5–18.
48 See e.g. *Militär-Wochenblatt*, 11 April 1927, 1412; 25 June 1928, 1893–5; 18 Sept. 1929, 401–3; 11 July 1930, 1816–7; *Kriegs-Gedanken aus dem Auslande*, 5 (1929), 8:11–16. Parts of Swinton's *Eyewitness* (1932), on the origins of the tank, were translated by German intelligence and circulated in typescript: RH 8/v. 1936–7; also see RH 8/v. 1935.
49 See *Wehrgedanken des Auslandes* (the journal's new title from 1931 on), 14 (1934); after 1930, when the novelty wore off somewhat, their dominating share in the journal declined.
50 Quotations respectively from *Militär-Wochenblatt*, 18 July 1926, 87; 25 Jan. 1927, 1027; 4 Nov. 1928, 675.

51 11/1948/38; Bond, *LH*, 234.
52 Geyer, 'German Strategy in the Age of Machine Warfare, 1914–1945', in Paret (ed.), *Makers of Modern Strategy*, 559; Nehring, *Panzerwaffe*, 54–6; also Wilhelm Deist in MF (ed.), *Germany and the Second World War*, i. 383–4.
53 In.6 (K) (signed Lutz), 1 and 18 June 1929, in RH 39/115.
54 T4 (signed Blomberg), 1 Sept. 1929, in RH 39/115. See also Geyer, 'German Strategy', 559.
55 Ogorkiewicz, *Armoured Forces*, 17–18, 87. The American copying of the British manoeuvres (and the influence of Fuller and Liddell Hart) is revealed on the basis of the documents by John Hendrix, 'The Interwar Army and Mechanization: The American Approach', *Journal of Strategic Studies*, 16 (1993), 77–81. As in Britain, General Douglas MacArthur, chief of staff of the US Army, finally decided to disband the experimental armoured force, and in the mid-1930s he opted for the mechanization of the whole army. In any case, LH did not exaggerate when he pointed out that MacArthur's 1935 Annual Report, emphasizing the coming of a mechanized battlefield, was unmistakably littered with LH's distinctive ideas and concepts: *The Times*, 22 Nov. 1935; LH, *The Tanks*, i. 271–2; *Memoirs*, i. 354–5.
56 See the official history, based on the documents: Lucio Ceva and Andrea Curami, *La Meccanizzazione dell'esercito italiano dalle origini al 1943* (Rome, 1989), 113–32.
57 Erickson, *The Soviet High Command* (London, 1962), 263–70; Simpkin, *Deep Battle*, 38 and *passim*; Gat, *Fascist and Liberal Visions of War*, 114–21.
58 For obvious reasons, too, LH wrote misleadingly in his *Memoirs*, i. 171–2, that they had discussed *Sherman*; cf. his records at the time: 7 and 8 Mar. 1932, in 11/1932/1 and 11/1932/9; this has been pointed out by Mearsheimer, *LH*, 162–3. See also Robert M. Citino, *The Evolution of Blitzkrieg Tactics: Germany Defends Itself against Poland 1918–1933* (London, 1987).
59 Reichenau to LH, 28 Nov. 1932, 9/24/87/R.
60 Thorne to Hankey, 22 March 1946, 13/45; Bond, *LH*, 219.
61 Guderian, *Panzer Leader*, 29, 37, 48. For a comprehensive discussion of the interrelationship between politics, strategy and mechanized warfare with respect to the pivotal role played by Blomberg and Reichenau, see my *Fascist and Liberal Visions of War*, 90–103.
62 Geyer, 'German Strategy, 1914–1945', in Paret (ed.), *Makers of Modern Strategy*, 558.
63 Guderian, *Panzer Leader*, 19–22; idem, 'Truppen auf Kraftwagen und Flieger-abwehr', *Militär-Wochenblatt*, 25 Sept. 1924, 305–6; 'Strassenpanzerkraftwagen und ihre Abwehr', *Der Kampfwagen*, 1 (Oct. 1924), 5–8; 'Aufklärung und Sicherung bei Kraftwagenmärschen', *ibid.*, 2 (Nov. 1924), 13–16; 'Die Lebensader Verduns', *ibid.*, 4 (Jan. 1925), 28–31, 'Kavallerie und Strassenpanzerkraftwagen', *ibid.*, 5 (Feb. 1925), 37–8. The backwardness and esoteric nature of these contributions have been pointed out by Corum, *Seeckt and German Military Reform*, 139.
64 Guderian, *Panzer Leader*, 21.
65 *Ibid.* 20.

66 *Ibid.*; however, it probably summarizes his development over a number of years from 1924 on. Martel, for example, was occasionally cited in German periodicals in the second half of the 1920s, especially in connection with his one-man tank, but it was only with the publication of his *In the Wake of the Tank* (1931; German tr. the same year) that his full significance for the development of armour theory as early as the First World War became clear.
67 Guderian to LH, 19 March 1949, 9/24/62.
68 Guderian, *Panzer Leader*, 20.
69 *Ibid.* 21–2.
70 *Ibid.* 22; Guderian first saw a real tank either during a visit to Sweden in 1929 (p. 23) or, perhaps, in connection with the clandestine German production.
71 Major Guderian, 'Bewegliche Truppenkörper. Eine kriegsgeschichtliche Studie', *Militär-Wochenblatt*, 11, 18, 25 Nov., 4, 11, Dec. 1927, 649–53, 687–94, 728–31, 772–6, 819–22. See also Bradley, *Generaloberst Heinz Guderian und die Entstehungsgeschichte des modernen Blitzkrieges* (Osnabruck, 1978), 166.
72 *Panzer Leader*, 24.
73 *Ibid.* 29, 31.
74 Sharp criticism of Guderian's egocentrism is expressed by Corum, *Seeckt and German Military Reform*, esp. 137–9; Corum, however, overstates a good case not only by unconvincingly claiming for Seeckt the crown of military innovation but also by blurring the difference between the Reichswehr's early attention to tanks which went along conventional lines and the new ideas developed from the mid-1920s under British influence. Guderian's cursory references to Volckheim and Heigl in *Panzer Leader*, 20–1, is in this respect understandable. On this see the balanced judgement of S.J. Lewis, *Forgotten Legions: German Army Infantry Policy 1918–1941* (New York, 1985), 18.
75 Michael Geyer, 'Das zweite Rustungsprogramm (1930–1934)', *Militärgeschichtliche Mitteilungen* 17 (1975), 25–72; Deist in MF (ed.), *Germany and the Second World War*, i. 395–9.
76 The tactical problem in *Militär-Wochenblatt*, 18 and 25 Jan. 1931, 1200–4, 1237–43 (signed Lieutenant Wedel); for various (unofficial) British proposals for the organization of an armoured division see *ibid.*, 11 July 1930, 1816–17; 25 June 1931, 1893–4.
77 *Militär-Wochenblatt*, 25 April 1931, 1561–4 (signed 'Crisolli'). For a similar comparison see *ibid.*, 25 Oct. 1933, 509–11 (signed '400'): 'a few years ago, mainly under the leadership of General Fuller, Britain built independent mechanized troops ...'
78 *Ibid.*, 25 Sept., 4 Oct. 1931, 433–9, 469–74 (signed '82'). In due course a similar survey specified the new 16 Tonner as the model for the modern medium tank: *ibid.*, 25 June 1934, 1659–62 (signed '143').
79 *Ibid.*, 11 and 18 Dec. 1932, 721–4, 756–61 (signed Lieutenant Faber du Faur).
80 *Ibid.*, 4 May 1933, 1340–3 (signed '349').
81 *Ibid.*, 25 July, 11 Aug., and 11 Nov. 1931, 139, 223, 661–2; quotation from 661.

82 *Ibid.*, 4 May 1933, 1340–3 (signed '349').
83 *Ibid.*, 25 June 1933, 1566–7 (signed Major-General Zölss).
84 *Ibid.*, 11 April 1934, 1259–62 (signed M. Braun).
85 Major Nehring, *Kampfwagen an die Front! Geschichte und neuzeitliche Entwicklung des Kampfwagens ('Tanks') im Auslande* (Leipzig, 1934), 20–1; there is no need to dwell on the difficulty of translating the German *operativ*, standing in an intermediate position between the English 'strategy' and 'tactics' and signifying combat strategy in the theatre of operations.
86 'England. Die Manöver der Kampfwagentruppen, Sommer 1932', 32 pp., 16 May 1933, copies in RH 2/2968 and RHD 18/137; noted by W. Heinemann, 'The Development of German Armoured Forces 1918–1940', in Harris and Toase (eds), *Armoured Warfare*, 53. Much of the material for the years 1932–34, contained in RH 2 and RH 12, is reportedly missing; but see the file by T3, 'Motorization and Mechanization in Britain at the Beginning of 1931', 15 pp. plus pictures, 10 Feb. and 20 March 1931, RH 12–6/v. 22; *The Daily Telegraph* is among the sources cited; there are similar surveys of Poland, France and Czechoslovakia.
87 His memoirs, Freiherr Geyer von Schweppenburg, *Erinnerungen eines Militärattachés, London 1933–1937* (Stuttgart, 1949), focus mainly on the political-strategic aspect of his mission.
88 4 May 1933, RH 2/1881; all reports sent to T3. On 20 July 1933 Geyer reported that there would be no concentration of the armour units that year.
89 T3, *ibid.*, 26 Oct. 1933; Geyer's report itself (30 Sept. 1933) is apparently missing.
90 19 March 1934, in RH 2/1882, quotation from p. 8.
91 10 Oct. 1934, in RH 2/1882, 15 pp. plus many sketches and appendixes.
92 *Militär-Wochenblatt*, 4 Oct. 1934, 489–94, quotation from 492 (signed '366'); also *ibid.*, 25 Oct. 1934, 610–16.
93 *Ibid.*, 25 Dec. 1935, 1056 (source not cited).
94 'England. Manöver des Panzerverbandes 18 bis 21.9.1934', Dec. 1934, 36 pp. plus appendixes and sketches, copies in RH 2/1442 and RHD 18/394.
95 For Fuller see e.g. *Militär-Wochenblatt*, 11 July 1931, 53–4; 18 Nov. 1932, 617–21; 4 March 1933, 1085–9; *Wehrgedanken des Auslandes*, 7 (1931), 3:5–13; 9 (1933), 12:4–13. For LH see e.g. reports in *The Daily Telegraph*, *Militär-Wochenblatt*, 11 Jan. and 25 May 1932, 951, 1558; also *ibid.*, 4 Jan. 1932, 1056–7; 25 April 1933, 1316–17; 11 Jan. 1934, 859–61; *Wehrgedanken des Auslandes*, 7 (1931), 9:11–12; 8 (1932), 4:29–30, 9:42–3. Criticism of Fuller and LH from *RUSI Journal*, *ibid.*, 7 (1931), 10:23–7.
96 The extracts came without references, but see almost certainly *Militär-Wochenblatt*, 25 Jan. 1932, 1014–15, for Fuller's *Grant*, and 11 April 1932, 1356, for LH; there are other almost certain examples before.
97 See e.g. Eimannsberger, *Der Kampfwagen Krieg*, 110; G.P. von Zezschwitz, *Heigls Taschenbuch der Tanks*, iii (Berlin, 1938), *passim.*; Nehring, *Kampfwagen an die Front!*, 20, all identifying the British school with Fuller who is the sole authority they cite. In Nehring, *Heere von Morgen. Ein Beitrag zur Frage der Heeresmotorisierung des Auslandes* (3rd edn.; Potsdam, 1935), 9, 28–9, Liddell Hart is presented as Fuller's partner; the conclusion is: 'The actual impact of the inspired enlightening work of these two

British officers can be seen in the series of instructive exercises conducted by the British high command in the last four years, which may offer a valuable clue for the armament of a modern army.'
98 Fuller's retirement was reported by *Militär-Wochenblatt*, 4 Feb. 1934, 966; a review of the issue of the *RUSI Journal* which honoured him on his retirement described him as 'the spiritual father of all the ideas of army mechanization of the time. His post-war books *The Reformation of War* and *Tanks in the Great War* won international reputation.... The British owe him gratitude for organizing the Royal Tank Corps and for the introduction of the Vickers Medium Tank in 1923': *ibid.*, 25 May 1934, 1525.
99 LH's article appeared in *The Daily Telegraph*, 3 Oct. 1933; Geyer's covering letter is dated 5 Oct.; both in RH 2/1881. His original report (no. 7) is registered in, but presently missing from, the file in the BA-MA. LH's article was summarized in *Militär-Wochenblatt*, 18 Dec. 1933, 761.
100 23 April 1934, in RH 2/1882.
101 14 Nov. 1934, in RH 2/1882.
102 23 April, 2 and 8 May 1935, in RH 2/1883; on 5 Jan. 1935 Geyer reported the appearance of the second edn of Martel, *In the Wake of the Tank*. When *Britain Goes to War* is commonly assumed to be merely a revised edition of LH's *The British Way in Warfare*; in fact, apart from the famous opening piece and a number of general essays on the theory of war, this is an entirely new book, incorporating many of LH's articles of the years 1931–35 on the manoeuvres of the British armoured forces, and constituting perhaps his most important book on the subject of armoured warfare.
103 *Militär-Wochenblatt*, 18 Jan. 1936, 1209–10 (signed Captain Schenk). The important chapter, 'The Future of Armament – and Its Future Use', was translated in *Wehrgedanken des Auslandes*, 11 (1935), 11:17–26. For a lengthy review of the book when it appeared in German ('great reading value'), by the editor of *Militär-Wochenblatt*, General Wetzell, see *ibid.*, 11 June 1937, 3037–41.
104 'Überblick über Manöver fremder Heere im Jahre 1935', *Militärwissenschaftliche Rundschau*, 1 (1936), 261–83; most of the article is on the French manoeuvre with their new mechanized formations, also *Militär-Wochenblatt* see 11 Nov. 1935, 756–60.
105 14 Oct. 1935, 20 pp. plus many appendixes, including a sketch of the Tank Brigade's manoeuvre of deep penetration.
106 Abt. III (formerly T3), 'Truppenübungen und Erfahrungen des englischen Heeres 1935', Nov. 1935, 45 pp. plus maps, in RH 2/1443, quotations from 5, 10; further citations from LH: 3, 6, 14, 30. Cf. the first chapter above, n. 41.
107 Hankey to LH, 27 Dec. 1933, 1/352, probably referring to the British military attaché.
108 For Geyer's correspondence with Berlin see 15 July 1935, in RH 2/1883; LH's own file of correspondence with Geyer is 9/24/61; invitations were discussed on 10 Aug. 1935, 14 Feb., 16 and 27 May 1936, cited by Bond, *LH*, 216, but not by Mearsheimer.
109 Talk with Thorne, 3 June 1942, 11/1942/41; Guderian, *Panzer Leader*, 35.
110 Paret to LH, 8 Oct. 1958, in 1/566; he heard it from his father who reportedly heard it either from professor Meinencke or from Sauerbruch.
111 Guderian, *Achtung Panzer*, 167.

112 Nehring, *Kampfwagen an die Front!*, 28.
113 Cited from the British cabinet papers by Brian Bond and Williamson Murray, 'The British Armed Forces', in A.R. Millett and W. Murray, *Military Effectiveness* (London, 1988), ii. 112.
114 Guderian, *Panzer Leader*, 32.
115 For the political aspect see my *Fascist and Liberal Visions of War*, 90–103.
116 Erich von Manstein, *Aus einem Soldatenleben 1887–1939* (Bonn, 1958), 128–9, 240–3.
117 Hubertus Senff, *Die Entwicklung der Panzerwaffe im deutschen Heer zwischen den beiden Weltkriegen* (Frankfurt a. M., 1969), 23–6; Nicholas Reynolds, *Treason Was No Crime: Ludwig Beck, Chief of the German General Staff*, 103–5; Deist in MF (ed.), *Germany and the Second World War*, i. 431–6; Klaus-Jürgen Müller, *General Ludwig Beck, Studien und Dokumente zur politisch-militärischen Vorstellungswelt und Tätigkeit des Generalstabschefs des deutschen Heeres 1933–1938* (Boppard, 1980), esp. 208–19; idem, *The Army, Politics and Society in Germany 1933–45* (Manchester, 1987), 54–99; Lewis, *Forgotten Legions*, xiii-xiv, 51–3.
118 This is rightly pointed out by Corum, *Seeckt and German Military Reform*, 199.
119 Heeresdienstvorschrift 300: *Truppenführung*, i (1933), paragraphs 339–40, pp. 133–5; ii (1934), paragraphs 725–58, pp. 1–10. See also Reynolds, *Beck*, 104, which despite its general sloppiness is the most perceptive about the development of Beck's attitude to armour.
120 Manstein, *Aus einem Soldatenleben*, 241.
121 'England. Manöver des Panzerverbandes 18 bis 21.9.1934', Dec. 1934, copies in RH 2/1442 and RHD 18/394; extracts from the report are printed in Müller, *Beck*, 360–6; see also Reynolds, *Beck*, 104–5.
122 Quoted by Reynolds, *Beck*, 106.
123 Beck, 'Nachträgliche Betrachtungen zu dem Einsatz des Panzerkorps in der Lage der Truppenamtsreise vom 13.6.1935', 25 July 1935: RH 2/v. 134; printed in Müller, *Beck*, 460–5. See also Reynolds, *Beck*, 105; Guderian, *Panzer Leader*, 32.
124 Kommando der Panzertruppen, 'Erfahrungsbericht über die Versuchsübungen einer Panzerdivision auf dem Truppenübungsplatz Münster im August 1935', 24 Dec. 1935, RHD 26/2.
125 'Erwägungen über die Erhöhung der Angriffskraft des Heeres', 30 Dec. 1935, in RH 2/1135; printed in Müller, *Beck*, 469–77; see also Reynolds, *Beck*, 105; and RH 2/1224.
126 See e.g. LH's comprehensive article on the future development of the British army in the *English Review*, summarized in *Militär-Wochenblatt*, 25 Aug. 1935, 315–16, and described as a 'highly interesting study'. The French manoeuvres were covered by a couple of articles in *Militär-Wochenblatt* in late 1935, and more extensively in 'Überblick über Manöver fremder Heere im Jahre 1935', *Militärwissenschaftliche Rundschau*, 1 (1936), 261–83.
127 The letter by the Allgemeines Heeresamt is dated 22 Jan. 1936, and Beck's reply, 30 Jan., both in RH 2/1135, the latter printed in Müller, *Beck*, 486–90; quotation from 488; more references to other countries, 487; and specifically to the French infantry tanks and motorized infantry divisions:

114 Notes

487, 489. Again on the three roles of armour see 23 and 25 March 1936, in RH 2/1135.
128 See the correspondence between Abt. I, II, IV, VIII, and Kdo. der Panzertruppen, in 5 (and no day) May, 3, 15, 17, 18, 29 June, and August (no day) 1936: all in RH 2/1135; 2 May 1936, in RH 2/1382.
129 Guderian, 'Schnelle Truppen einst und jetzt', *Militärwissenschaftliche Rundschau*, 4 (1939), 240–1. See also idem, *Panzer Leader*, 36; Manstein, *Aus einem Soldatenleben*, 242.
130 Müller, *Beck*, esp. 474; idem, *The Army, Politics and Society*, 85.
131 See Abt II, 13 Aug. 1936, in RH 2/1135, and cf. Guderian, 'Die Panzertruppen und ihr Zusammenwirken mit den anderen Waffen', *Militärwissenschaftliche Rundschau*, 1 (1936), 614–15 (citing Fuller, *The Army in My Time*); reissued separately in book form the following year.
132 Beck had already raised the issue in his 30 Dec. 1935 memorandum, in RH 2/1135, printed in Müller, *Beck*, 472. For his decision in the affirmative see Abt II, 5 and 12 Oct. 1936, in RH 2/1135.
133 Manstein, *Aus einem Soldatenleben*, 243ff.
134 In mid-1936, during his own battle against the infantry tank, Guderian criticized the British decision – in divergence from their traditional policy – to attach a tank battalion to each infantry division, in addition to the creation of the Mobile Division. (The decision must have been waved in his face in Germany.) He argued that the split would weaken the armoured force and that British tanks were anyhow too fast and light for the infantry support role. He was apparently not yet aware of the British intention to produce a special slow and heavily armoured infantry tank, an idea, of course, which he did not like either: 'Die Panzertruppen und ihr Zusammenwirken mit den anderen Waffen', *Militärwissenschaftliche Rundschau*, 1 (1936), 614–15.
135 This distinction was first developed with regard to the British army by Winton, *To Change an Army*.
136 *Militär-Wochenblatt*, 11 July 1932 (signed Lieutenant Freytag).
137 Nehring, *Kampfwagen an die Front!*, 25–6; also idem, *Heere von Morgen*, 38–40, citing the Soviet theorist Isserson (Moscow, 1932); Nehring's book on anti-tank warfare, *Panzerabwehr* (2nd edn.; Berlin, 1937), also cites Soviet sources and views, including Tukhachevsky's.
138 Heigls, *Taschenbuch der Tanks* (2 vols; Munich, 1935), ii. 455–7.
139 M.J. Kurtzinski (ed. and tr.), *Taktik Schneller Verbände* (Potsdam, 1935).
140 14 March 1935, in RH 2/1438; 1 April 1936, in RH 2/1439; 14 Sept. 1936 and 8 April 1937, in RH 2/1444.
141 *Militär-Wochenblatt*, 11 Oct. 1936, 720–1 (from *The Times*); 18 Oct. 1936, 776–7; 11 Dec. 1936, 1188–93; 22 Jan. 1937, 1589–92. A translated article on artillery in 'deep battle' was published ibid., 25 Dec. 1936, 1332–5.
142 'Operative und taktische Grundsätze sowjetrussischer Kriegsführung', *Militärwissenschaftliche Rundschau*, 3 (1938), 557–74, 671–86. See also Max Werner, *The Military Strength of the Powers* (London, 1939), 106–16 and *passim*.
143 Guderian to LH, 24 Jan. 1949, in 9/24/62, mistakenly dating the visit to 1933; Nehring, *Panzerwaffe*, 42–6; Zeidler, *Reichswehr und Rote Armee*, 196.
144 Guderian, 'Kraftfahrkampftruppen', *Militärwissenschaftliche Rundschau*, 1 (1936), 73, citing Kryshanowski; also *Achtung Panzer!*, 151–4.

145 Nehring, *Kampfwagen an die Front!*, 26; Guderian, *Achtung Panzer!*, 153; idem, 'Schnelle Truppen einst und jetzt', *Militärwissenschaftliche Rundschau*, 4 (1939), 237–8. The German criticism of the Soviet armour doctrine in the 1930s has been well noted by Senff, *Die Entwicklung der Panzerwaffe*, 22.
146 For the radio see Macksey, *Guderian*, 50–1, 67.
147 Guderian, *Panzer Leader*, 38, 46; Nehring, *Panzerwaffe*, 93; the material relating to the manoeuvres can be found in RHD 18/296–8, RHD 18/357–8; the detailed report of Major-General A.C. Temperley on the manoeuvre and the state of the Panzer arm for *The Daily Telegraph* and *Morning Post* was translated into German and sent to Berlin by the German military attaché in London: RH 53–7/v. 54.
148 See esp. F.O. Miksche, *Blitzkrieg* (London, 1942); Klaus Maier's contribution to MF (ed.), *Germany and the Second World War*, ii (Oxford, 1991), 41–3.
149 RH 2/2930.
150 RH 2/1437–41.
151 *Militär-Wochenblatt*, 25 Nov. and 4 Dec. 1936, 1059–63, 1108–10; for the armour see 1109–10.
152 Ibid., 22 Oct. 1937, 1053; also 29 Oct., 1117–18.
153 Zina Hugo to LH, 28 Oct. 1941, 13/5 miscellaneous file, also 11/1948/38; cited by Bond *LH*, 230, but not by Mearsheimer. See also LH, *The Other Side of the Hill*, 65–6.
154 The Thoma file 1 Nov. 1945, 9/24/144; Guderian to General Dittmar, 29 Aug. 1948; Guderian to LH, 7 Oct. 1948 and 19 Mar. 1949: all in 9/24/62; none cited by Mearsheimer, but see Bond, *LH*, 229–31.
155 Guderian to LH, 19 March 1949, 9/24/62.
156 LH to Chester Wilmot, 14 May 1953, 9/24/30; cited by Mearsheimer, *LH*, 161.
157 Macksey, *Guderian*, 41; *The Tank Pioneers*, 118; Mearsheimer, *LH*, 165–6. Guderian, *Achtung Panzer!*, 141, cites Fuller, Martel and Liddell Hart, in that order, as the pioneers of the idea of an all-arms armoured formation.
158 Macksey, *The Tank Pioneers*, 118.
159 Fuller, *Memoirs*; Swinton, *Eyewitness*; Martel, *In the Wake of the Tank*.
160 Guderian, *Achtung Panzer!*, 141, also 170.
161 Macksey, *Guderian*, 69.
162 *The Army Quarterly* (August 1942), 216, cited in Fuller, *Armoured Warfare*, 5.
163 For Fuller fascist-charged writings see e.g. *Militär-Wochenblatt*, 25 Dec. 1936, 1312–14; 21 May 1937, 2836; 9 July 1937, 65–7; *Wehrgedanken des Auslandes*, 13 (1937), 2:13–21, 7–8:5–13; 14 (1938), 7–8:5–12, 12:6–9; 15 (1939), 2:29–30, 7–8:14–19. For his visits to Germany and the German use of his political writings see Trythall, *Fuller*, 184, 187, 192, 203.
164 Quoted in Macksey, *Guderian*, 41. For the Fuller–Guderian meeting see also Trythall, *Fuller*, 203.
165 Guderian's son was himself a junior officer in the Panzer force in the late 1930s, but he was not his father, there are the problems of the distance of time and of the inquirer's leading questions, and there is the weight of other evidence of the time.

166 See e.g. *Militär-Wochenblatt*, 20 April 1936, 1756–9 (signed '326'); 11 June 1937, 3066–7; 29 Oct. 1937, 1117–18 (quotation; signed '326'); cf. this translation from the German summary with the original in *The Times*: the first chapter above n. 46–8 and related text. See also the intelligence translation: Abt. III, 12 April 1937, RH 2/1440.
167 Larry Addington, *The Blitzkrieg Era and the German General Staff, 1865–1941* (New Brunswick N.J., 1971), *passim*; Michael Geyer, *Aufrüstung oder Sicherheit. Die Reichswehr in der Krise der Machtpolitik 1924–1936* (Wiesbaden, 1980), 481; Carver, *The Apostles of Mobility*, 63–4; Daniel J. Hughes, 'Abuses of German Military History', *Military Review* (Dec. 1986), 69–70; also, somewhat along these lines, Mearsheimer, *LH*, 87, 92. For the argument that 'Blitzkrieg' diverged from the traditional German emphasis on battles of annihilation see Matthew Cooper, *The German Army 1933–1945* (London, 1978), 130–48 and *passim*; Mearsheimer, *Conventional Deterrence*, 38–9; Barry Posen, *The Sources of Military Doctrine: France, Britain, and Germany between the World Wars* (London, 1984), 86, 206–7.
168 Guderian, *Panzer Leader*, 316.
169 Michael Geyer's hyperbolic claim that 'Blitzkrieg' was defined as an operational design only in hindsight and with some help from Liddell Hart is basically correct: Geyer, 'German Strategy', in Paret (ed.), *Makers of Modern Strategy*, 585–6; also Manfred Messerschmidt, 'The Political and Strategic Significance of Advances in Armament Technology: Developments in Germany and the "Strategy of Blitzkrieg"', in R. Ahmann, A. M. Birke and M. Howard (eds), *The Quest for Stability* (Oxford, 1993), 249–61; J. P. Harris, 'The Myth of Blitzkrieg', *War in History*, 2 (1995), 335–52, repeating, however, the erroneous claims about LH's lack of influence.
170 *Militär-Wochenblatt*, July 1940, 165; Guderian, *Panzer Leader*, 461. For LH see *The Defence of Britain*, 101.
171 For the debate on Hitler's 'economic Blitzkrieg' see: A.S. Milward, *The German Economy in War* (London, 1965); R.J. Overy, *War and Economy in the Third Reich* (Oxford, 1994).
172 Robert O'Neill, *The German Army and the Nazi Party* (London, 1966), 127.
173 Quoted without reference by Macksey, *Guderian*, 59.
174 Nehring, *Heere von Morgen*, 31.
175 Guderian, *Panzer Leader*, esp. 92, 159, 166–9, 182, 185, 199; Guderian to LH, 24 Jan. 1949, 9/24/62.
176 Germains had anticipated this criticism in his *The 'Mechanization' of War*, 178. For North Africa see the opinions of Rommel and Bayerlein, *The Rommel Papers*, 159, 184. Michael Carver, *Tobruk* (London, 1964), esp. 254–5 lays much of the blame on LH's teachings; also Shelford Bidwell, *Gunners at War* (London, 1970), 163–82. In his reply to Carver LH cleverly threw the blame on the 'cavalry mentality' of many of the newly converted British armour commanders: *The Times Literary Supplement*, 19 Nov. 1964.
177 *Militär-Wochenblatt*, 6 Feb. 1942, 918; for the original see *This Expanding War*, 171 (18 Jan. 1942).
178 See again Dec. 1934 in RH 2/1442, cited in Müller, *Beck*, 361.
179 See e.g. Nehring, *Kampfwagen an die Front!*, 18–19.

180 Guderian, 'Schnelle Truppen einst und jetzt', *Militärwissenschaftliche Rundschau*, 4, 243.
181 Cited without reference in Ogorkiewicz, *Armoured Forces*, 21.
182 See e.g. Nehring, *Heere von Morgen*, Bibliography, 9, 33–5; *idem*, *Panzerabwehr*, 53; Guderian, 'Kraftfahrkampftruppen', *Militärwissenschaftliche Rundschau*, 1 (1936), 71; *idem*, 'Die Panzertruppen und ihr Zusammenwirken mit den anderen Waffen', *ibid.*, 616–17, 619; *idem*, *Achtung Panzer!*, 150, Bibliography.
183 Quoted in Trythall, *Fuller*, 209–10. For André Beaufre's recollections of the effect of LH's writings on the younger generation of French officers see Michael Howard (ed.), *The Theory and Practice of War* (London, 1965), 138–41; cf. Alexander, *Gamelin*, 242–3.
184 Eimannsberger, *Der Kampfwagen Krieg* (Berlin, 1934), 109–10, 167.
185 *Ibid.*, 113–209.
186 *Ibid.*, 170–209.
187 *Ibid.*, 161–9.
188 Dermont Bradley, *Generaloberst Heinz Guderian und die Entstehungsgeschichte des modernen Blitzkrieges* 2, 184–7, solicited the evidence of some of the Panzer arm's veterans. The verdict was shared by all of them, including Nehring, whose works in the 1930s regularly referred to Eimannsberger among the other authorities cited: Nehring, *Heere von Morgen*, Source List and 43–4; *Panzerabwehr*, 13.
189 In the second edition of his book (1938) Eimannsberger introduced a number of other changes to conform to the divisional structures actually adopted by the Wehrmacht. Mikshe, relying on this edition, mistakenly believed that these were Eimannsberger's original proposals of 1934, thus forming an exaggerated idea of his potential influence: *Blitzkrieg*, 107–9.
190 For material relating to the first manoeuvres of the Panzer divisions see RHD 26/2–5.
191 *Ibid.*; Guderian, 'Kraftfahrkampftruppen', *Militärwissenschaftliche Rundschau*, 1 (1936), 68; *idem*, *Achtung Panzer!*, 143; the whole thing was rightly pointed out by Ogorkiewicz, *Armoured Forces*, 43–4, 57–8, 79.
192 In addition to the reports mentioned above see e.g. Nehring, *Heere von Morgen*, 32–3, 72–3; Guderian, 'Kraftfahrkampfwagen', 68–9. Again the German modelling on the British has been discerned by Ogorkiewicz, *Armoured Forces*, 72–3.
193 Guderian, *Achtung Panzer!*, 141.
194 Quoted in Macksey, *Guderian*, 59.
195 Summary of *Paris* in *Kriegs-Gedanken aus dem Auslande* 2 (1926), 8:23–6; 'The Remaking of Modern armies', in *The Daily Telegraph*, *ibid.*, 3 (1927) 3:18–23.
196 A review article of the book ('the well known Captain Liddell Hart'): 'novel, surprising proposals, some of which are already implemented in experimental units': *Militär-Wochenblatt*, 11 Jan. 1934, 859–61; also *ibid.*, 4 Oct. 1934, 513. For the book's resonance in Germany: *ibid.*, 18 Jan. 1936, 1209; Nehring, *Heere von Morgen*, Bibliography and 15. The book influenced Felix Steiner, a battalion and regiment commander in the Waffen SS and developer of training methods for infantry: Bernd Wegner, *The Waffen SS: Organization, Ideology and Function* (Oxford, 1990), 184. That the book

had in fact little to say on armoured infantry has been noted by Reid, *Fuller*, 161.
197 See W. Velten, *Das deutsche Reichsheer und die Grundlagen seiner Truppenführung* (Munster, 1982); and the persistent emphasis in the training instructions issued by the Command of the Panzer Troops: RHD 26/2 (24 Dec. 1935), RHD 26/3 (10 Nov. 1935), RHD 26/4 (10 Nov. 1936), RHD 26/5 (15 Nov. 1937); also Guderian, *Achtung Panzer!*, 178ff and *passim*.
198 For LH's views on the subject see e.g. *Militär-Wochenblatt*, 25 Aug. 1935, 315–16; and of course in the translated *When Britain Goes to War*.
199 Guderian, *Panzer Leader*, 37.
200 The expected reduction in the tank establishment of the British armoured division from its earlier very high level was noted by Guderian on the eve of the war: 'Schnelle Truppen einst und jetzt', *Militärwissenschaftliche Rundschau* 4 (1939), 238.
201 See e.g. Frido von Senger und Etterlin, *Neither Fear Nor Hope* (London, 1960; foreword by LH), 79–80.
202 Guderian, *Panzer Leader*, 294–5; the first chapter, n. 145 above.
203 26 May and 15 June 1942, *The Rommel Papers*, 203.
204 Again see my *Fascist and Liberal Visions of War*.

Select Bibliography

Archives

Liddell Hart Centre for Military Archives, King's College, London.
Bundesarchiv-Militärarchiv, Freiburg im Breisgau.

Books and Articles
(excluding newspaper writings and selective on periodical articles)

Addington, Larry, *The Blitzkrieg Era and the German General Staff, 1865–1941* (New Brunswick, NJ, 1971).
Alexander, Martin, 'Maurice Gamelin', in Brian Bond (ed.), *Fallen Stars, Eleven Studies of Twentieth Century Military Disasters* (London, 1991).
——, *The Republic in Danger: General Maurice Gamelin and the Politics of French Defence, 1933–1940* (Cambridge, 1992).
Barnett, Correlli (ed.), *Hitler's Generals* (London, 1989).
Beaufre, André, 'Liddell Hart and the French Army, 1919–1939', in Michael Howard (ed.), *The Theory and Practice of War* (London, 1965).
Bidwell, Shelford, *Gunners at War* (London, 1970).
Bond, Brian, *France and Belgium, 1939–1940* (London, 1975).
——, *Liddell Hart: a Study of His Military Thought* (London, 1977).
——, *British Military Policy between the Two World Wars* (Oxford, 1980).
—— and Williamson Murray, 'The British Armed Forces', in A.R. Millett and W. Murray, *Military Effectiveness* (London, 1988), ii. 98–130.
Bradley, Dermont, *Generaloberst Heinz Guderian und die Entstehungsgeschichte des modernen Blitzkrieges* (Osnabrück, 1978).
Carver, Michael, *Tobruk* (London, 1964).
——, *The Apostles of Mobility* (London, 1979).
Ceva, Lucio, and Andrea Curami, *La Meccanizzazione dell'esercito italiano dalle origini al 1943* (Rome, 1989).
Churchill, Winston, *The Second World War* (6 vols; London, 1948–55).
Citino, Robert M., *The Evolution of Blitzkrieg Tactics: Germany Defends Itself against Poland 1918–1933* (London, 1987).
Cooper, Matthew, *The German Army 1933–1945* (London, 1978).
Corum, James S., *The Roots of Blitzkrieg: Hans von Seeckt and German Military Reform* (Lawrence, Kans., 1992).
Danchev, Alex, *Alchemist of War: the Life of Basil Liddell Hart* (London, 1998).
De Gaulle, Charles, *Vers l'armée de métier* (Paris, 1934).
Doughty, Robert A., *The Seeds of Disaster: The Development of French Army Doctrine 1919–1939* (Hamden, CT, 1985).
——, *The Breaking Point: Sedan and the Fall of France, 1940* (Hamden, CT, 1990).
Dutailly, Henry, *Les Problèmes de l'armée de terre française (1935–1939)* (Paris, 1980).
Eimannsberger, Ludwig Ritter von, *Der Kampfwagen Krieg* (Berlin, 1934).
Erickson, John, *The Soviet High Command* (London, 1962).
Fuller, John Frederick Charles, 'Gold Medal (Military) Prize Essay for 1919:

"The Application of Recent Developments in Mechanics and Other Scientific Knowledge to Preparation and Training for Future War on Land"', *RUSI Journal*, 65 (1920), 239–74.
——, *Tanks in the Great War 1914–1918* (London, 1920).
——, *The Reformation of War* (London, 1923)
——, *On Future Warfare* (London, 1928).
——, 'One Hundred Problems of Mechanization', Part Two, *The Army Quarterly*, 19 (1929).
——, *Armoured Warfare* (London, 1943; originally *Lectures on FSR III*, 1932).
——, *Memoirs of an Unconventional Soldier* (London, 1936).
——, 'The Problem of Tank and Anti-Tank Weapons', *The Fighting Forces*, 14 (1937).
——, *Towards Armageddon* (London, 1937).
——, *Watchwords* (London, 1944).
Gat, Azar, *Fascist and Liberal Visions of War: Fuller, Liddell Hart, Douhet and Other Modernists* (Oxford, 1998).
Germains, Victor, *The 'Mechanization' of War* (London, 1927).
Geyer, Michael, 'Das zweite Rustungsprogramm (1930-1934)', *Militärgeschichtliche Mitteilungen* 17 (1975), 25–72.
——, *Aufrüstung oder Sicherheit. Die Reichswehr in der Krise der Machtpolitik 1924–1936* (Wiesbaden, 1980).
——, 'German Strategy in the Age of Machine Warfare, 1914–1945', in Paret (ed.), *Makers of Modern Strategy* (Princeton, 1986), 527–97.
Gibbs, Norman, *Grand Strategy*, i (London, 1976).
Guderian, Heinz, *Achtung Panzer! The Development of Armoured Forces, Their Tactics and Operational Potential* (London, 1992; German original 1937).
——, *Die Panzertruppen, und ihr Zusammenwirken mit den anderen Waffen* (Berlin, 1937).
——, 'Schnelle Truppen einst und jetzt', *Militärwissenschaftliche Rundschau*, 4 (1939).
——, *Panzer Leader* (London, 1952); German original *Erinnerungen eines Soldaten* (Heidelberg, 1951).
Gunsburg, Jeffery A., *Divided and Conquered: the French High Command and the Defeat of the West, 1940* (London, 1979).
Harris, J. Paul, 'Sir Percy Hobart', in Brian Bond (ed.), *Fallen Stars, Eleven Studies of Twentieth Century Military Disasters* (London, 1991), 86–106.
——, *Men, Ideas and Tanks: British Military Thought and Armoured Forces, 1903–1939* (Manchester, 1995).
——, 'The Myth of Blitzkrieg', *War in History*, 2 (1995), 335–52.
—— and F.H. Toase (eds), *Armoured Warfare* (London, 1990).
Heeresdienstvorschrift 487, *Führung und Gefecht der verbundenen Waffen* (Berlin, 1923).
Heeresdienstvorschrift 300: *Truppenführung*, two vols (1933, 1934).
Heigl, Fritz, *Taschenbuch der Tanks* (Munich, 1926); expanded posthumous edns, 1935, 1938.
Hendrix, John, 'The Interwar Army and Mechanization: The American Approach', *Journal of Strategic Studies*, 16 (1993), 77–81.
Higham, Robin, *The Military Intellectuals in Britain 1918–1939* (New Brunswick, NJ, 1966).

Hinsley, F.H., *British Intelligence in the Second World War*, i (London, 1979).
Hughes, Daniel J., 'Abuses of German Military History', *Military Review* (Dec. 1986).
Ironside, Edmund, *The Ironside Diaries, 1937-1940* (London, 1962), edited by Roderick Macleod and Denis Kelly.
Kurtzinski, M.J. (ed. and tr.), *Taktik Schneller Verbände* (Potsdam, 1935).
Larson, Robert, *The British Army and the Theory of Armoured Warfare 1918-1940* (Newark, Delaware, 1984).
Leeb, Ritter von, *Defence* (Harisburg, Pa., 1943).
Lewis, S.J., *Forgotten Legions: German Army Infantry Policy 1918-1941* ((New York, 1985).
Liddell Hart, Basil Henry, 'Suggestions on the Future Development of the Combat Unit – the Tank as a Weapon of Infantry', *RUSI Journal* (Nov. 1919), 666-9.
——, 'The Next Great War', *The Royal Engineers Journal* (March 1924), 90-107.
——, 'The Development of the "New Model" Army, Suggestions on a Progressive, but Gradual Mechanization', *The Army Quarterly* (Oct. 1924), 37-50.
——, *Paris, or the Future of War* (London, 1925).
——, *The Remaking of Modern Armies* (London, 1927).
——, *Great Captains Unveiled* (London, 1927).
——, 'Armoured Forces in 1928', *RUSI Journal* (Dec. 1928).
——, *Sherman* (London, 1929).
——, *The Decisive Wars of History* (London, 1929); later renamed *Strategy: the Indirect Approach*.
——, 'The New British Doctrine of Mechanized War', *The English Review* (Dec. 1929).
——, 'The Future of Armament and Its Future Use', *Yale Review* (June 1930).
——, 'The Army Exercises of 1930', *RUSI Journal* (Nov. 1930), 681-90.
——, *The Real War* (London, 1930); expanded and reissued as *A History of the World War* (London, 1934).
——, *Foch: the man of Orlean* (London, 1931).
——, 'Contrasts of 1931, Mobility or Stagnation', *Army Quarterly* (Jan. 1932).
——, *When Britain Goes to War* (London, 1935).
——, *Europe in Arms* (London, 1937).
——, *The Defence of Britain* (London, 1939).
——, *Dynamic Defence* (London, 1940).
——, *The Current of War* (London, 1941).
——, *This Expanding War* (London, 1942).
——, *Thoughts on War* (London, 1944).
——, *The Revolution in Warfare* (London, 1946).
——, *The Other Side of the Hill* (London, 1948).
——, *Defence of the West* (London, 1950).
——, *The Tanks* (London, 1959).
——, *Deterrent or Defence* (London, 1960)
——, *The Memoirs of Captain Liddell Hart* (London, 1965).
'Liddell Hart: the Captain Who Taught Generals', *The Listener*, 28 Dec. 1972.
Luvaas, Jay, *The Education of an Army: British Military Thought, 1815-1940* (London, 1965).

Macksey, Kenneth, *Armoured Crusader: a Biography of Major General Sir Percy Hobart* (London, 1967).
——, *Guderian: Panzer General* (London, 1975).
——, *The Tank Pioneers* (London, 1981).
Manstein, Erich von, *Aus einem Soldatenleben 1887–1939* (Bonn, 1958).
——, *Lost Victories* (London, 1958)
Martel, Giffard le Q., *In the Wake of the Tank* (London, 1931).
——, *An Outspoken Soldier* (London, 1949).
Mearsheimer, John, *Conventional Deterrence* (Ithaca and London, 1983).
——, *Liddell Hart and the Weight of History* (London, 1988).
Messerschmidt, Manfred, 'The Political and Strategic Significance of Advances in Armament Technology: Developments in Germany and the "Strategy of Blitzkrieg"', in R. Ahmann, A.M. Birke and M. Howard (eds), *The Quest for Stability* (Oxford, 1993), 249–61.
Miksche, F.O., *Blitzkrieg* (London, 1942).
Militärgeschichtliches Forschungsamt (ed.), *Germany in the Second World War* (Oxford, 1990–).
Milward, A.S., *The German Economy in War* (London, 1965).
Müller, Klaus-Jürgen, *General Ludwig Beck. Studien und Dokumente zur politisch-militärischen Vorstellungswelt und Tätigkeit des Generalstabschefs des deutschen Heeres 1933–1938* (Boppard, 1980).
——, *The Army, Politics and Society in Germany 1933–45* (Manchester, 1987).
Nehring, Walter, *Kampfwagen an die Front! Geschichte und neuzeitliche Entwicklung des Kampfwagens ('Tanks') im Auslande* (Leipzig, 1934).
——, *Heere von Morgen. Ein Beitrag zur Frage der Heeresmotorisierung des Auslandes* (3rd edn; Potsdam, 1935).
——, *Panzerabwehr* (2nd edn; Berlin, 1937).
——, *Die Geschichte der deutschen Panzerwaffe, 1916 bis 1945* (Berlin, 1969).
Ogorkiewicz, R.M., *Armoured Forces* (London, 1970).
O'Neill, Robert, *The German Army and the Nazi Party* (London, 1966).
Oswald, Werner, *Kraftfahrzeuge und Panzer der Reichswehr, Wehrmacht und Bundeswehr* (Stuttgart, 1982).
Overy, R.J., *War and Economy in the Third Reich* (Oxford, 1994).
Paget, Reginald, *Manstein: His Campaigns and His Trials* (London, 1951).
Paillat, Claude, *Le Désastre de 1940* (2 vols; Paris, 1983, 1984).
Posen, Barry, *The Sources of Military Doctrine: France, Britain, and Germany between the World Wars* (London, 1984).
Reid, Brian Holden, *J.F.C. Fuller: Military Thinker* (London, 1987).
Reynolds, Nicholas, *Treason was no Crime: Ludwig Beck, Chief of the German General Staff* (London, 1976).
Rommel, Erwin, *The Rommel Papers* (London, 1953), edited by B.H. Liddell Hart.
Schweppenburg, Freiherr Geyer von, *Erinnerungen eines Militärattachés, London 1933–1937* (Stuttgart, 1949).
Senff, Hubertus, *Die Entwicklung der Panzerwaffe im deutschen Heer zwischen den beiden Weltkriegen* (Frankfurt a. M., 1969).
Senger und Etterlin, Frido von, *Neither Fear Nor Hope* (London, 1960), foreword by Liddell Hart.
Simpkin, Richard, *Deep Battle: the Brainchild of Marshal Tukhachevski* (London, 1987).

Spielberger, Walter, *Die Motorisierung der deutschen Reichswehr 1920-1935* (Stuttgart, 1979).
Swinton, Ernest, *Eyewitness* (London, 1932).
Trythal, A.J., *'Boney' Fuller: the Intellectual General* (London, 1977).
Velten, W., *Das deutsche Reichsheer und die Grundlagen seiner Truppenführung* (Munster, 1982).
Volckheim, Ernst, *Die deutschen Kampfwagen im Weltkrieg* (Berlin, 1923).
——, *Der Kampfwagen in der heutigen Kriegsführung* (Berlin, 1924).
——, *Wissen and Wehr* (Berlin, 1924).
——, *Betrachtungen über Kampfwagen-Organisation und Verwendung. Zu einer Abhandlung des englischen Majors Sherbrooke* (Berlin, 1924).
——, *Kampfwagen und Abwehr dagegen* (Berlin, 1925).
Young, Robert, *In Command of France: French Foreign Policy and Military Planning 1933–1940* (Cambridge Mass., 1978).
——, 'French Military Intelligence and Nazi Germany, 1938–1939', in Ernest R. May (ed.), *Knowing One's Enemies: Intelligence Assessment before the Two World Wars* (Princeton, 1984).
The War Office, *Mechanized and Armoured Formations* (1929); revised as *Modern Formations* (1931).
Wark, K., *The Ultimate Enemy: British Intelligence and Nazi Germany, 1933–1939* (London, 1985).
Wegner, Bernd, *The Waffen SS: Organization, Ideology and Function* (Oxford, 1990).
Werner, Max, *The Military Strength of the Powers* (London, 1939).
Wheldon, John, *Machine Age Armies* (London, 1968).
Winton, Harold, *To Change an Army: General Sir John Burnett-Stuart and British Armoured Doctrine, 1927–1938* (Lawrence, Kans., 1988; doctoral diss. 1977).
Zeidler, Manfred, *Reichswehr und Rote Armee 1920-1933* (Munich, 1993).

Index

Adam, Ronald, 30
Adam, Wilhelm, 63
Alléhaud, General, 86

Bayerlein, Fritz, 45
Beaufre, André, 117 n. 183
Beck, Ludwig, 63, 67, 68–74, 76, 83, 85, 93–4, 101 n.85
Blitzkrieg, 82–5
Blomberg, Werner, 53, 56–8, 60, 68, 93
Blumentritt, Günther, 56
Bond, Brian, 6
Broad, Charles, 7, 9, 13, 15, 17–18, 37, 55, 62, 71
Brooke, Alan, 16, 40
Burnett-Stuart, John, 98 n.43

Camon, Hubert, 86
Chamberlain, Neville, 24
Churchill, Winston, 30, 41, 86, 90, 99 n.65

Daladier, Éduard, 24
Daly, T. Denis, 81
Davis, D., 57
De Gaulle, Charles, 80, 86
Deverell, Cyrill, 23, 27, 38, 77
Dill, John, 67
Douhet, Giulio, vi

Eden, Anthony, 90
Eimannsberger, Ludwig, Ritter von, 86–7
Elles, Hugh, 74, 101 n.90

Fritsch, Werner von, 54, 60, 68, 93
Fromm, Fritz, 72
Fuller, John Fredrick Charles, vi, vii, 1–5, 6, 7, 13–15, 19, 20, 29, 35–7, 42, 45, 46, 47, 48, 50, 51, 52, 53, 55, 56, 57, 58, 59, 60, 64, 66, 67, 70, 75, 78, 80, 81, 82, 86, 88, 90, 91–5

Gamelin, Maurice, 24, 30
Germains, Victor, 21, 99 n.54, 108 n.47
Geyer von Schweppenburg, Leo Freiherr, 63–7, 70, 77, 94
Gort, Lord, 23, 26, 30
Guderian, Heinz, vi, 40, 42, 44, 45–7, 48, 49, 51, 55, 58, 59–61, 62, 67, 68, 69, 70, 72–3, 76, 78–9, 80, 81, 82, 83, 84–6, 88, 89, 90, 94, 100 n.72, 116 n.176

Haining, R.H., 23
Halder, Franz, 29
Hankey, Maurice, 66
Heigl, Fritz, 50, 75
Hess, Rudolf, 81
Heye, Wilhelm, 54, 60, 93
Hitler, Adolf, 42, 46, 58, 61, 68, 81, 84, 90, 93
Hobart, Percy, 9–10, 11, 12, 13, 15–17, 25, 38–42, 55, 64–5, 77, 78, 79, 80, 81, 87, 92, 94
Hore-Belisha, Lesley, 23, 38, 39

Ironside, Edmund, 24

Khandeyeff, Colonel, 78–9, 80
Knox, Harry, 23

Leeb, Ritter von, 29
Liddell Hart, Basil Henry, vi, vii, 1–42, 43–8, 50–1, 52, 53, 54, 55, 56, 57, 58, 59, 64–7, 70, 77–9, 80, 81, 82, 83, 85, 86, 88, 89, 90, 91–5
Lindsay, George, 13, 15–17, 37–8, 87, 91
Lutz, Oswald, 56, 61, 62, 67, 71, 76
Luvaas, Jay, 6

Macksey, Kenneth, 47, 79–80, 81
Manstein, Erich von, 29, 44, 68–9, 70, 73

Martel, Giffard le Q., 13, 14, 15, 41, 46, 47, 55, 59, 74, 76, 80, 88, 91, 93, 101 n.90, 110 n.66
Maxe, Ivor, 2
Mearsheimer, John, vii, 1, 5–6, 11, 14, 18, 24, 44, 46, 79
Milne, George, 7, 53, 54
Mongol strategy and tactics, 6, 7, 8, 15, 16
Montgomery-Massingberd, Archibald, 10

Namier, Louis, 105 n.2
Napoleon I, 83
Nehring, Walter, 62, 67, 75, 76, 84

Paget, Bernard, 30–1
Paret, Peter, 67
Pile, Fredrick 'Tim', 13, 52

Reichenau, Walter, 57–8, 68

Ribbentrop, Joachim von, 81
Richmond, Herbert, 55
Robertson, William, 55
Rommel, Erwin, 44, 45, 90, 94, 103 n.116
Rowan-Robinson, Colonel, 55
Rundstedt, Gerd von, 101 n.85

Seeckt, Hans von, 49, 54
Sherman, William T., 6, 8, 15
Swinton, Ernest, 55, 79, 80

Temperley, A.C., 115 n.147
Thoma, Wilhelm von, 78–9
Thorne, Andrew, 57, 67
Tukhachevsky, Mikhael, 22, 100 n.72

Volckheim, Ernst, 49–50, 59

Wells, H.G., 2